THE ANGLO-IRISH AGREEMENT

Commentary, Text and Official Review

AUSTRALIA AND NEW ZEALAND
The Law Book Company Ltd.
Sydney : Melbourne : Perth

CANADA AND U.S.A.
The Carswell Company Ltd.
Agincourt, Ontario

INDIA
N.M. Tripathi Private Ltd.
Bombay
and
Eastern Law House Private Ltd.
Calcutta and Delhi
M.P.P. House
Bangalore

ISRAEL
Steimatzky's Agency Ltd.
Jerusalem : Tel Aviv : Haifa

PAKISTAN
Pakistan Law House
Karachi

THE ANGLO-IRISH AGREEMENT

Commentary, Text and Official Review

BY

Tom Hadden
(Professor of Law at Queen's University, Belfast)
and
Kevin Boyle
(Professor of Law at the University of Essex)

Edwin Higel Ltd

Sweet & Maxwell Ltd

Published in 1989 by
Sweet & Maxwell Limited of
South Quay Plaza, 183 Marsh Wall
London E14 9FT
in association with
Edwin Higel Limited
2 Brookside, Dundrum Road
Dublin 14, Ireland.
Computerset by Promenade Graphics Limited, Cheltenham.
Printed in Scotland.

British Library Cataloguing in Publication Data
Hadden, Tom
    The Anglo-Irish Agreement: commentary, text and official review.
    1. Northern Ireland. Government. Treaties: Anglo-Irish
    Agreement
    I. Title II. Boyle, Kevin
    341.4' 2

ISBN 0–421–42660–8

Preface

This commentary was completed early in 1989 and submitted to the United Kingdom and Irish Governments in the context of the review of the Agreement under Article 11. It contains comments on events and legislation up to the end of 1988. The text of the Official Review, which was finally published in May 1989, has been added in Chapter 7 without further commentary.

Acknowledgements

We should like to acknowledge the assistance of the Nuffield Foundation who made a Small Grant of £2,800 for research assistance and to meet other expenses. This enabled us to obtain the assistance of George Ruddell and Colm Campbell. George Ruddell was responsible not only for the collection of materials on all parts of the Agreement and for the preparation of the final typescript, but also for the whole of the chapter on the International Fund for Ireland (Chapter 3). Without his meticulous research and unflagging energy we could not have embarked on such a thorough commentary. Colm Campbell was responsible for the whole of Chapter 4 on Extradition and we are grateful to him for permission to make use of his research on individual extradition cases. Many others whom it would be invidious either to name or not to name have assisted us by commenting on drafts at various stages in our work. We are grateful to them all, even though we have not been able to accept all their suggestions or criticisms.

Contents

	PAGE
Preface	v
Acknowledgements	vi

1. INTRODUCTION ... 1

1. *The Background to the Agreement* ... 1
   Conflicting claims ... 1
   The Sunningdale Conference ... 2
   The failure of the Sunningdale package ... 3
   The Anglo-Irish Joint Studies of 1981 ... 4
   The Anglo-Irish Intergovernmental Council ... 5
   Anglo-Irish Encounter ... 5
   The New Ireland Forum ... 6
   The preparation of the Agreement ... 8
2. *The Agreement* ... 9
   General structure ... 9
   Status in international law ... 11
   Status in national law ... 12
   Political nature of the Agreement ... 14

2. ANNOTATION OF THE AGREEMENT ... 15

   Preamble ... 15
   Article 1 ... 18
   Article 2 ... 22
   Article 3 ... 26
   Article 4 ... 28
   Article 5 ... 30
   Article 6 ... 34
   Article 7 ... 35
   Article 8 ... 38
   Article 9 ... 40
   Article 10 ... 42
   Article 11 ... 46
   Article 12 ... 47
   Article 13 ... 48

3. THE INTERNATIONAL FUND FOR IRELAND ... 49

   Introductory note ... 49
   Annotation of Agreement ... 51
   Conclusion ... 57

4. EXTRADITION ... 59

   1970–1976: strict application of political offence exception ... 59

Contents

1976–1982: the Sunningdale compromise on extra-territorial
jurisdiction   60
1982–1987: judicial re-interpretation of the political offence
exception in Ireland   61
1987 to date: The European Convention on the Suppression of
Terrorism and the Irish legislation of 1987   63

5. REACTIONS AND ACHIEVEMENTS   67

Political reaction   67
Opinion polls   71
Achievements   72

6. FUTURE DEVELOPMENTS   76

The objectives of the Agreement   76
Restoring the momentum of the Agreement   77
Interim changes   78
Accommodating full unionist participation   80

7. THE OFFICIAL REVIEW OF THE AGREEMENT   83

Index   89

CHAPTER 1

INTRODUCTION

The Anglo-Irish Agreement was signed on November 15, 1985 at Hillsborough, County Down between the Government of the United Kingdom of Great Britain and Northern Ireland and the Government of Ireland.* In Britain a motion supporting the Agreement was passed by the House of Commons by 473 votes to 47 on November 27, 1985 and by the House of Lords on November 26, 1985 (No voting figures were recorded). In Ireland a similar motion was passed by Dáil Éireann by 88 votes to 75 on November 21, 1985 and by Seanad Éireann by 37 votes to 16 on November 28, 1985. It was lodged at the United Nations on November 28, 1985 and entered into force on November 29, 1985 when notifications of acceptance were exchanged by the two Governments (see Article 13). Though there are some differences in the descriptions of the parties to the Agreement in the versions signed respectively by the two Governments, as discussed below, the operative terms of the Agreement are identical in both versions. These differences are also observable in the versions officially published in Britain (Cmnd. 9690) and in the Irish Republic (Prl. 3684).

1. THE BACKGROUND TO THE AGREEMENT

Conflicting claims

The Agreement represents the most significant and carefully prepared development in the relationship between Britain and Ireland since the partition settlement of the 1920s. This relationship reached a low ebb during the 1930s and 1940s. In the early 1930s the two countries became involved in a trade war. In 1937 Ireland adopted a new Constitution (Bunreacht na hÉireann) which asserted a form of jurisdiction over the whole island of Ireland. In 1948, under the Republic of Ireland Act, it declared itself to be a republic and left the British Commonwealth. The United Kingdom responded by enacting the Ireland Act 1949 which asserted exclusive British jurisdiction over Northern Ireland.

These conflicting constitutional claims were progressively set aside as economic relations were redeveloped in the post-war years. Though the trade war had been partially resolved in the Trade Agreements of 1938 (Cmd. 5728), 1948 (Cmd. 7504) and 1960 (Cmnd. 1019) it was not until 1965 that full freedom of trade between the two countries was re-established under the Free Trade Area Agreement (Cmnd. 2858). In 1973 both countries joined the European Community.

The outbreak of disturbances in Northern Ireland in 1968, however, caused renewed strains on this developing comity. The initial reaction of the British Government was to treat the problem of Northern Ireland as an exclusively internal affair and to reject as interference concern expressed by other countries, notably Ireland. The Irish Government, however, continued to assert its concern over developments in Northern Ireland. For example, in August 1969 the Taoiseach, Jack Lynch, publicly stated that " . . . the Irish Government can no longer stand by and see innocent people injured and, perhaps, worse. The Irish Government have . . . requested

* Throughout this report we have used the full and correct titles of the two states—*i.e. The United Kingdom of Great Britain and Northern Ireland* and *Ireland*—except where brevity or the context required otherwise. This is in pursuit of our recommendation that in all their dealings, whether bilateral or multilateral, the two states should do likewise and thus avoid the continuing and sometimes damaging use of separate titles in British and Irish versions of treaties, communiques and other governmental statements.

the British Government to apply immediately to the United Nations for the urgent despatch of a peace-keeping force to the six counties of Northern Ireland . . . " [*Belfast Telegraph*, August 14, 1969]. The British Government responded in the United Nations by asserting that "Northern Ireland had long been an integral part of the United Kingdom and that events there were an internal matter for the U.K. Government" [August 20, 1969 *per* Lord Caradon, U.K. permanent representative; see *Keesing's Contemporary Archives* (1969), 23584 A].

The Sunningdale Conference

After the suspension of the devolved Northern Ireland government in March 1972 and the introduction of direct rule from Westminster the importance of the Irish dimension in dealing with Northern Ireland was eventually accepted by the British Government. The first formal attempt to build a settlement of the Northern Ireland problem on a joint British-Irish basis was made at the Sunningdale Conference in December 1973, at which representatives of both unionist and nationalist parties in Northern Ireland agreed with the British and Irish Governments on a package of measures to deal with the relations between Northern Ireland and Ireland and the internal government of Northern Ireland. Though the Sunningdale agreement was no more than an agreed communique, many of its terms may be seen as direct precedents for those of the 1985 Agreement and it was envisaged that some at least of its content would be incorporated in a formal agreement between the British and Irish Governments and registered at the United Nations (Communique, para. 6).

(i) *The status of Northern Ireland*

The first significant element of the Sunningdale communique was a series of statements on the aspirations of the parties and on the status of Northern Ireland. The Irish Government and the Social Democratic and Labour Party (SDLP) delegation asserted their aspiration towards a united Ireland and that they wished to achieve unity only by consent (para. 3). The Unionist and Alliance Party delegations asserted the firm desire of the majority of the people of Northern Ireland to remain part of the United Kingdom (para. 4). The Irish and British Governments made the following parallel declarations (para. 5):

The Irish Government fully accepted and solemnly declared that there could be no change in the status of Northern Ireland until a majority of the people in Northern Ireland desired a change in that status.	The British Government solemnly declared that it was, and would remain, their policy to support the wishes of the majority of the people in Northern Ireland. The present status of Northern Ireland is that it is part of the United Kingdom. If in the future the majority of the people of Northern Ireland should indicate a wish to become part of a united Ireland, the British Government would support that wish.

It may be noted in comparison with the terms of the 1985 Agreement that the Irish Government did not make any declaration as to what the current status of Northern Ireland was, and that the British Government, while asserting clearly what that status was, committed themselves only to supporting self-determination for the people of Northern Ireland in choosing either continued membership of the United Kingdom or a united Ireland.

(ii) *The Council of Ireland*

The second element in the Sunningdale agreement was the setting up of a Council of Ireland to deal with certain matters on a joint basis between the two parts of Ireland. Such a Council was provided for under the

Government of Ireland Act 1920 (s.2(1)) but had never been established since different arrangements for the government of Southern Ireland were made under the 1921 Treaty. Under the Sunningdale agreement the Council was to comprise a Council of Ministers with seven members from the Northern Ireland Executive and seven from the Irish Government, a Secretariat and a Consultative Assembly with 30 members from the Northern Ireland Assembly and 30 from Dáil Éireann. The Council was to have both harmonising and executive functions, the latter to be identified by studies of a wide range of economic and environmental matters. The cost of the Secretariat was to be shared equally by Northern Ireland and Ireland and the cost of any jointly-operated services in proportion to the benefit enjoyed. The Council was also to have a role in the development of human rights protections and in the appointment of police authorities in both parts of Ireland. It may be noted in comparison with the terms of the 1985 Agreement in respect of the ministerial conference that the Council of Ireland was envisaged as a North/South body with reciprocal powers and duties in both parts of Ireland and that the British Government was to be involved only in so far as it might be necessary to protect its financial interests while it continued to pay a subsidy to Northern Ireland.

(iii) *Power-sharing Executive*

The third element in the Sunningdale agreement was the understanding that Northern Ireland was to be governed by a "power-sharing Executive" on which agreement had already been reached in discussions with the Secretary of State for Northern Ireland and some but not all the political parties in Northern Ireland. The representatives of the Unionist, Alliance and Social Democratic and Labour Parties took part in the Sunningdale Conference in their capacity as members designate of the proposed Northern Ireland Executive.

(iv) *Co-operation on terrorism*

The final element in the Sunningdale agreement was the recognition that the battle against terrorism was an all-Ireland concern, and that this might involve the operation of a common law enforcement area, the creation of an all-Ireland court for certain purposes and new arrangements for extradition or extra-territorial jurisdiction in respect of terrorist offenders. Detailed discussion of the legal complexities involved was to be left to an expert commission which eventually reported in 1974 (see below). It was envisaged in this context that internment without trial would be phased out and that the increase in communal confidence in Northern Ireland as the power-sharing Executive settled in might permit the devolution of normal policing powers.

The failure of the Sunningdale package

Very little of this elaborate package was ever implemented. No formal agreement was entered into or registered at the United Nations as promised in the communique. This was due in part to the challenge by opponents of the agreement in Ireland to the constitutionality of the declaration by the Irish Government on the status of Northern Ireland on the ground that it conflicted with the provisions of Articles 2 and 3 of the Irish Constitution. The Irish Supreme Court held that the declaration amounted at most to a statement of policy rather than a formal recognition of the current status of Northern Ireland as part of the United Kingdom; but some of the judges indicated that a formal agreement that Northern Ireland was part of the United Kingdom as opposed to a statement of policy on any change in its status might be repugnant to the Constitution and might be challenged if and when the executive sought to give it formal legal effect (*Boland* v. *An Taoiseach* [1974] I. R. 338).

Nor was any progress made towards the establishment of a Council of Ireland. Opponents of the Sunningdale agreement in Northern Ireland portrayed the proposed Council of Ireland as a major step towards Irish unification and used the arguments of the Irish Government in the *Boland* case as further evidence that no real recognition of the status of Northern Ireland had been granted. In the British General Election of February 1974 opponents of Sunningdale were elected in 11 of the 12 Northern Ireland constituencies and there were increasing political difficulties within the power-sharing Executive over the proposed Council of Ireland. The Executive was eventually forced to resign by a political strike organised by the Ulster Workers Council in May 1974 to oppose the formation of a Council of Ireland in any form.

The only lasting achievement of the Sunningdale Conference resulted from the report of the commission of senior judges from Britain, Northern Ireland and Ireland on extradition and related matters (*Report of the Law Enforcement Commission*, 1974, Cmnd. 5627, Prl. 3832). Though agreement could not be reached on new rules for the extradition of political offenders, which the representatives of Ireland argued would be contrary to international law and the Irish Constitution, the report recommended the adoption of broader procedures for the exercise of extra-territorial jurisdiction in such cases. Legislation to this effect was introduced in the United Kingdom under the Criminal Jurisdiction Act 1975 and in Ireland under the Criminal Law (Jurisdiction) Act 1976.

The Anglo-Irish Joint Studies of 1981

From 1974 until 1980 a number of attempts were made to promote an internal political settlement within Northern Ireland. But little progress was made, due largely to the continuing differences between the major unionist and nationalist parties over the issues of power-sharing and the "Irish dimension." The possibility of making greater progress at an inter-state level re-emerged at a summit meeting between Mrs Thatcher and Mr Haughey on May 21, 1980, at which agreement was recorded on the importance of the

"unique relationship between the peoples of the United Kingdom of Great Britain and Northern Ireland and the Republic and on the need to further this relationship in the interests of peace and reconciliation."

At a further summit meeting on December 8, 1980 it was agreed that special consideration should be given during 1981 to "the totality of relationships within these islands" and a number of joint studies covering possible new institutional relationships, citizenship rights, security matters, economic co-operation and measures to encourage mutual understanding were commissioned.

These joint studies were pursued at official level during 1981. Final reports were presented on November 2, 1981 and laid before both Parliaments on November 11, 1981 (Cmnd. 8414 and Pl. 299). The joint study on *Possible New Institutional Structures* explored possible forms for new Anglo-Irish institutions at various levels. The first suggestion was for the formalisation of existing patterns of contact at ministerial and official level in an Anglo-Irish Intergovernmental Council. It was also suggested that an Anglo-Irish Ministerial Council might be established without the need for legislation, perhaps by a formal intergovernmental agreement. It was suggested that a Secretariat for any new body might be composed of designated officials from each Government, and that it might be appropriate for a complementary inter-parliamentary body to be developed. Finally, it was suggested that it might be appropriate to create an Advisory Committee on economic, social and cultural co-operation, which would be associated with the proposed Council but independent of governments or parliaments; as an interim measure wider economic, social and cultural exchanges might be promoted by a body to be called Anglo-Irish Encounter modelled on the Koenigswinter Conference. Detailed joint studies were also made on *Citizenship Rights*, *Economic Co-operation* and *Measures to Encourage Mutual Understanding*. It was agreed that the work of any new institutional structures should take place

> "within a constitutional framework in which the factual position of Northern Ireland could not be changed without the consent of the majority of the people of Northern Ireland and the agreement of Parliament at Westminster."

It is clear that many of the developments of the ensuing years may be traced back to these joint studies in 1981.

The Anglo-Irish Intergovernmental Council

Formal ministerial agreement to the creation of the Anglo-Irish Intergovernmental Council was recorded at the summit meeting between Mrs Thatcher and Dr Fitzgerald on November 6, 1981. Despite the suggestion in the Joint Studies, this was not followed by a formal agreement, but was merely reported to the British Parliament (H.C. Debs. (6th) cols. 422 ff (November 11, 1981)) and the Oireachtas (361 *Dáil Debates* cols. 1572 ff (November 11, 1981)). There does not appear, therefore, to be any formal constitution or rules of procedure for the Intergovernmental Council, which in one sense is merely a name for the continuing series of intergovernmental contacts at various levels. Thus the next summit meeting on November 7, 1983, again between Mrs Thatcher and Dr Fitzgerald, was described as the first meeting of the Anglo-Irish Intergovernmental Council at the level of Heads of Government. But it was reported in the Joint Report of the steering Committee of the Council that between January 1982, when the first ministerial and official meetings took place, and November 1983 twenty bilateral meetings within the framework of the Council had taken place; of these, six had been concerned with the Kinsale gas project and five had been between the Secretary of State for Northern Ireland and the Minister for Foreign Affairs on general Anglo-Irish relations (Pl. 1953).

Anglo-Irish Encounter

During this period the non-governmental Anglo-Irish Encounter recommended in the initial Joint Studies had also been established. Formal agreement on this was announced at the ministerial meeting between the Minister for Foreign Affairs and the Secretaries of State for Foreign and Commonwealth Affairs and Northern Ireland on July 27, 1983 and Dr T. K. Whitaker and Sir David Orr were appointed as joint chairmen. The first Anglo-Irish Encounter Conference was held on April 4, 1984 on the subject of improving work prospects in Britain and Ireland. Since then the following series of half yearly conferences have been held:

November 27–28, 1984, Dublin—
Theme: The promotion amongst the young of a greater respect for religious and cultural diversity.

March 26–27, 1985, London—
Theme: Increasing the appreciation of our cultural heritage.

September 20–22, 1985, Oxford—
Theme: The promotion of Irish Studies in Britain.

November 26–27, 1985, Dublin—
Theme: The role of the churches in British-Irish relationships.

March 19, 1986, London—
Theme: The Role of the Media.

May 16–18, 1986, Dublin—
Theme: Youth Exchanges.

November 25–26, 1986, Dublin—
Theme: The abuse of alcohol and other drugs.

April 8–9, 1987, London—
Theme: The promotion of economic growth through innovation and investment.

November 26–27, 1987, Dublin—
Theme: Britain, Ireland and the European Community.

March 4–6, 1988, Cardiff—
Theme: The future of Britain and Ireland in Europe (for young people).

November 15–16, 1988, Dublin—
Theme: The future of health care.

Copies of proceedings may be obtained from—

Anglo-Irish Encounter,
Institute of Public Administration,
57–61 Lansdowne Road,
DUBLIN 4

Anglo-Irish Encounter,
10 St James's Square,
LONDON,
SW1Y 4LE

The New Ireland Forum

While these initiatives were being pursued by the two Governments a renewed attempt was being made by nationalists in both parts of Ireland to redefine their attitudes to Irish unity. Both at the Sunningdale Conference and at successive summits the leaders of all major parties in Ireland had committed themselves to the pursuit of unification only with the consent of the majority of people in Northern Ireland and it was obvious that this could not be achieved without reassessing the Catholic and Gaelic tradition upon which the Irish state had long been based. There was also increasing concern in the aftermath of the hunger strikes of 1980 and 1981 that the Social Democratic and Labour Party, which was also committed to the pursuit of unification by consent, might be overtaken as effective representatives of the majority of nationalists in Northern Ireland by Provisional Sinn Féin, the political wing of the IRA. It was eventually agreed between John Hume, leader of the SDLP, and the leaders of the three main parties in Ireland, Fianna Fáil, Fine Gael and the Irish Labour Party, that a New Ireland Forum should be established with the express purpose of finding a way in which "lasting peace and stability could be achieved in a New Ireland through the democratic process." The unionist parties were invited but declined to participate.

The New Ireland Forum was convened in the summer of 1983 and heard evidence from a wide range of political and other groups. Its final Report in May 1984 stated that "a united Ireland in the form of a sovereign independent Irish state to be achieved peacefully and by consent" was "the best and most durable basis for peace and stability" (paras. 5.4 and 5.5). The preferred form of unity, in Mr Haughey's interpretation of the Report, was a unitary state which would "embrace the whole island of Ireland governed as a single unit under one government and one parliament elected by all the people of the island" (para. 6.1). But other leading participants laid equal stress on the two other options explored in detail, a federal or confederal state, and a system of joint authority under which the Governments in London and Dublin would share responsibility for the government of

Northern Ireland. The Report also included the offer to consider other ways in which the "realities and requirements" identified in the report—notably the need to accommodate both traditions in Northern Ireland—might be met. One of the most important of these was that "the political arrangements for a new and sovereign Ireland would have to be freely negotiated and agreed to by the people of the North and by the people of the South" (para. 5.2).

(i) *British Government reaction*

The response of the British Government to the *New Ireland Forum Report* in a debate in the House of Commons on July 2, 1984 was to reject the three main Forum options as unrealistic given the clearly expressed wishes of the majority of the people of Northern Ireland (63 H. C. Debs. (6th) col. 23). In the press conference following the summit meeting with Dr Fitzgerald on November 18–19, 1984 Mrs Thatcher used even harsher words: "The unified Ireland was one solution—that is out. A second solution was a confederation of the two States—that is out. A third solution was joint authority—that is out" (*Belfast Telegraph*, November 20, 1984). The joint communique of this summit meeting (referred to as the second meeting of the Anglo-Irish Intergovernmental Council at the level of Heads of Government) merely restated the position agreed at previous summit meetings: that the Irish Government wished the two parts of Ireland to come together by freely negotiated agreement and in peace, but recognised that any change in the constitutional status of Northern Ireland would only come about with the consent of a majority of the people of Northern Ireland; the Prime Minister reaffirmed that Northern Ireland was part of the United Kingdom, that the majority in Northern Ireland wanted it to remain so, and that if in the future the majority of the people of Northern Ireland clearly wished for and consented to a change in the constitutional status of Northern Ireland the United Kingdom Government would put forward and support legislation to that end. The work of the New Ireland Forum, however, was recognised in a further statement in the communique that "the identities of both the majority and the minority communities in Northern Ireland should be recognised and respected and reflected in the structures and processes of Northern Ireland in ways acceptable to both communities" and that "the process of government in Northern Ireland should be such as to provide the people of both communities with the confidence that their rights will be safeguarded."

(ii) *The Kilbrandon and Alliance Reports*

The *New Ireland Forum Report* was important in eliciting further responses. In Britain, the Kilbrandon Committee was established in 1984 as an unofficial body representative of the main strands in British and Northern Irish politics to make a broader response than was possible for the British Government. A majority on the Committee favoured a form of joint authority which it termed "co-operative devolution," and which would have resulted in the government of Northern Ireland by a five member ministerial executive comprising one British minister, one Irish minister, two unionist ministers and one Northern Ireland nationalist minister; but all its members accepted the need for some formal recognition of the legitimacy of Northern Ireland by Ireland (*Northern Ireland: Report of an Independent Inquiry*, November 1984). In the following year, the Liberal/Social Democratic Party Alliance produced a further set of proposals in the light of both the New Ireland Forum and the Kilbrandon Reports (*What Future for Northern Ireland?*, July 1985). This joint interparty commission, chaired by Lord Donaldson, rejected any form of joint authority as unacceptable to unionists and as a barrier to devolved self-government on a shared basis. It recommended instead a structure for legislative and executive devolution based on proportional representation. Individual ministers were to be elected under a proportional representation system by all members of a Northern Ireland Assembly and supervised by a series of parliamentary committees. The Irish dimension was to be supplied by creating a consultative and deliberative British-Irish Parliamentary Council, modelled on the Nordic Council, and a British-Irish Security Commission. In their broad structure, if not in all matters of detail, these Alliance proposals were significantly closer to what eventually emerged in the Anglo-Irish Agreement.

(iii) *The Unionist responses*

The Northern Ireland Assembly, which at the time represented only unionist opinion since the nationalist parties had refused to take up their seats, made its response through a series of reports from its Devolution Report Committee which had been established in February 1984, but which did not start work until June 1984. Its first Report incorporated documents from the main unionist parties which recognised the need for greater recognition of the rights and aspirations of the minority community, notably *The Way Forward* presented by the Ulster Unionist Party, and made suggestions for more effective scrutiny of government by Assembly Committees, and for the enactment of a Bill of Rights for Northern Ireland together with the establishment of a Human Rights Commission to assist in the enforcement of such a Bill (Northern Ireland Assembly 154, October 1984). Its second Report stressed its acceptance of the overriding principle that any scheme of government should command acceptance throughout the community and explored without commitment a number of proposals made to that end by witnesses before the Committee (Northern Ireland Assembly 182, February 1985). Its third Report, issued a few weeks before the signature of the Anglo-Irish Agreement, recommended serious and urgent consideration of the so-called Catherwood proposal under which the approval of a weighted majority of two-thirds of the members of the Northern Ireland Assembly would be required to support a devolved executive for an initial period of up to four years, thus in effect ensuring a form of power-sharing (Northern Ireland Assembly 225, October 1985).

The preparation of the Agreement

Despite the summary rejection by the British Government of its preferred options the work of the New Ireland Forum had a substantial impact on the drafting of the Anglo-Irish Agreement, which began in earnest soon after the summit meeting of November 1984. The preparation of the Agreement was restricted to a small body of officials and diplomats at the highest level both on the British and Irish sides. The Irish team was composed of Dermot Nally, Secretary to the Irish Government, Sean Donlon, Head of the Department of Foreign Affairs, Michael Lillis, also of the Department of Foreign Affairs, Noel Dorr, the Irish Ambassador in London, and, in the final stages, Andrew Ward, Secretary to the Department of Justice, and Declan Quigley, former legal adviser to the Irish Attorney-General. The British team was composed of Sir Robert Armstrong, the Secretary to the Cabinet, David Goodall, Deputy Secretary at the Cabinet Office and, later, at the Foreign and Commonwealth Office, Chris Mallaby, the new Deputy Secretary at the Cabinet Office, Sir Robert Andrew and Anthony Brennan of the Northern Ireland Office, and Sir Alan Goodison, the British Ambassador in Dublin. The ministers most directly involved on the Irish side were the Taoiseach, Dr Fitzgerald, Peter Barry, Minister for Foreign Affairs, Dick Spring, the Tánaiste, and the Attorney-General, John Rogers S.C. On the British side the ministers most directly involved were Douglas Hurd, Secretary of State for Northern Ireland, and Sir Geoffrey Howe, Foreign Secretary, though occasional informal summit meetings were held during various European Community meeting of Heads of Governments, notably at Milan on June 29, 1985. It also appears that a cabinet committee chaired by Lord Whitelaw was established to monitor progress. The negotiations were conducted with more than usual secrecy. It appears that the main points of the Agreement had been settled by the early autumn and indications of its content were conveyed informally to the Social Democratic and Labour Party and other interested politicians in Britain and Ireland. It is less clear to what extent Unionist leaders were kept informed. It was not until October 30 that James Molyneaux and Ian Paisley, the two Unionist party leaders, met Mrs Thatcher to express their opposition to the proposed agreement which had by that time been widely, if not entirely accurately, reported. By that time Douglas Hurd had been replaced as Secretary of State for Northern Ireland by Tom King. But this does not appear to have resulted in any major changes to the drafting of the Agreement.

2. THE AGREEMENT

The Anglo-Irish Agreement was eventually signed in Northern Ireland on November 15, 1985 at Hillsborough Castle, the former residence of the Governor-General of Northern Ireland before that position was abolished in 1973. The choice of this location and the presence in Northern Ireland of the Prime Minister, Mrs Thatcher, and of the Taoiseach, Dr Fitzgerald, each accompanied by a team of senior ministers was clearly intended to emphasise the new co-operative relationship between the United Kingdom and Ireland over the government of Northern Ireland.

General structure

The general structure of the Agreement and many of the particular provisions may be traced directly to the lengthy series of intergovernmental discussions and studies which have been summarised above, as well as to the Report of the New Ireland Forum (for a detailed account see B. Hadfield, "The Anglo-Irish Agreement 1985—Blue Print or Green Print?" (1986) *Northern Ireland Legal Quarterly* 1). This is clear from the following summary of the content of the Agreement:

The Preamble

This refers to the joint concern of the United Kingdom and Ireland as members of the European Community to achieve lasting peace and stability in Northern Ireland and to the need to recognise the existence of the two traditions and communities in Northern Ireland, and to accommodate both their respective aspirations and their rights to live in peace, to be free from any discrimination and to participate fully in the processes of government.

Section A: Status of Northern Ireland

Article 1 sets out the position of the two Governments as to the current situation and the need for majority consent within Northern Ireland for any change in status in similar terms to those adopted in the communiques of successive summits.

Section B: The Intergovernmental Conference

Articles 2 to 4 establish a new intergovernmental ministerial conference and secretariat through which the Government of Ireland may put forward views and proposals on a wide range of matters of government and administration in Northern Ireland without prejudice either to British sovereignty or to the objective of establishing a devolved government in Northern Ireland acceptable to both communities.

Section C: Political Matters

Articles 5 and 6 impose on the Conference a duty to promote measures to accommodate the rights and identities of both communities and recognises the right of the Irish Government pending devolution to represent the interests of the minority nationalist community within Northern Ireland.

Section D: Security and Related Matters

Article 7 sets out the role of the Conference on security, policing and prisons policy within Northern Ireland.

Section E: Legal Matters Including the Administration of Justice

Article 8 sets out the role of the Conference in respect of law enforcement and extradition in both parts of Ireland.

Section F: Cross-Border Co-operation on Security, Economic, Social and Cultural Matters

Articles 9 and 10 set out the role of the Conference on cross-border security co-operation, and on cross-border co-operation on other matters pending agreement on devolution; it also provides for intergovernmental co-operation and for the possibility of international support for economic and social development in areas most affected by the troubles.

Section G: Arrangements for Review

Article 11 provides for the review of the working of the Conference at the end of three years or earlier if either party requests.

Section H: Interparliamentary Relations

Article 12 provides for intergovernmental support for an Anglo-Irish Parliamentary body of the kind suggested in the Anglo-Irish Studies Report in 1981 if the two Parliaments so decide.

Section I: Final Clauses

Article 13 provides for the entry into force of the Agreement on exchange of notifications of acceptance.

Despite the complex structure of the Agreement and the very careful drafting of many of the individual provisions the objectives of those who drew it up can be summarised in simpler terms: first, to entrench the status of Northern Ireland as part of the United Kingdom until a majority of its people decide otherwise; secondly, to recognise the equal validity of both traditions in Northern Ireland; thirdly, to provide in the Anglo-Irish Conference a mechanism through which the Irish Government could represent the interests of the nationalist minority in Northern Ireland until such time as an agreement on devolution permitted representatives of that community within Northern Ireland to carry out that role for themselves; fourthly, to provide for cross-border co-operation on security and other matters, initially through the Conference and eventually between a devolved government in Northern Ireland and the Irish Government leaving a much smaller residual role for the Conference; and finally, to ensure that there was no conflict of sovereignty in the sense that ultimate responsibility for decision-making on either side of the border would remain with the United Kingdom and Irish Governments. Whether these objectives could be or have been successfully achieved under the Agreement as drafted will be discussed in greater detail below.

The status of the Agreement in international law

The Anglo-Irish Agreement is an interstate treaty governed by the ordinary rules of international law. As such it is not binding on either government in domestic law. And it is enforceable only in the sense that either side may ultimately seek a ruling on its effect at the International Court of Justice. This has been recognised by the courts in both countries. In an application by members of the Ulster Unionist Council in the High Court in London in November 1985 for leave to seek judicial review of the Agreement on the ground that the establishment of the Anglo-Irish Intergovernmental Conference was contrary to law it was held that the Agreement itself was "in the field of international relations"; "it concern[ed] relations between the United Kingdom and another sovereign state and it [was] not the function of the court to inquire into the exercise of the prerogative in entering into such an agreement or by way of anticipation to decide whether the method proposed of implementing the agreement [was] appropriate" (*Ex p. Molyneaux* [1986] 1 W. L. R. 331, at p. 336, *per* Taylor J.). Similarly in a challenge in the High Court in Dublin by two individual unionists to the constitutionality of the Agreement under the Irish Constitution it was held that "the Anglo-Irish Agreement is an international treaty and its only meaning is its meaning in international law" (*McGimpsey & McGimpsey* v. *Ireland* (unreported, High Court, July 29, 1988) *per* Barrington J.). The additional statement in the first of these cases that the Agreement was "akin to a treaty" must therefore be viewed as imprecise and misleading but excusable in an *ex tempore* judgment.

The Vienna Convention

As an international treaty the Anglo-Irish Agreement falls under the general rules set out in the Vienna Convention on the Law of Treaties of 1969, which sets out agreed international practice in the application and interpretation of treaties. The Convention has been signed and ratified by the United Kingdom (Cmnd. 4818) but not by Ireland. As noted by Barrington J. in *McGimpsey & McGimpsey* v. *Ireland* (unreported, High Court, July 29, 1988), however, some at least of its provisions are binding on Ireland as customary rules of international law.

There are a number of points of particular significance to the Anglo-Irish Agreement which are clarified under the Vienna Convention. First, it is clear that the Agreement as a treaty must be complied with in good faith notwithstanding anything to the contrary in the internal law of the state parties (Arts. 26 and 27). Though this obligation depends exclusively on international law, it may involve a change in the internal law of a state party. For this reason the entry into force of a treaty may be made expressly dependent on the enactment of any necessary legislation. This principle clearly applies with equal force to any constitutional provision in the case of Ireland. Thus, for example, the accession of Ireland to the Treaty of Rome was thought to require the adoption of a general constitutional amendment stating that "no provision of [the Irish Constitution] invalidates laws enacted, acts done or measures adopted by the State necessitated by the obligations of membership of the Communities or prevents laws enacted, acts done or measures adopted by the Communities, or institutions thereof, from having the force of law in the State" (Third Amendment of the Constitution Act 1972, Part II). The Supreme Court held on similar grounds that a referendum was necessary to alter the Irish Constitution before the Single European Act could be ratified (*Crotty* v. *An Taoiseach* [1987] I.L.R.M. 400). If any part of the Anglo-Irish Agreement were held to be unconstitutional in the current appeal proceedings in *McGimpsey & McGimpsey* v. *Ireland* (unreported, High Court, July 29,

1988), compliance with the Agreement would clearly require the adoption of an appropriate amendment to the Irish Constitution.

Secondly, it is clear that the terms of the Agreement must be interpreted in good faith in accordance with the ordinary meaning of the words used, their context and the objects and purposes of the treaty (Art. 31). For this purpose it is permissible to take into account the Preamble to the Agreement and also any preparatory materials. Though this latter term is not clearly defined it certainly includes any record of the negotiations which is available and perhaps also such "preparatory materials" as the *New Ireland Forum Report*, and the Anglo-Irish Joint Studies.

Thirdly, it is clear that under the Vienna Convention a treaty may be amended or modified at any time by the agreement of the parties unless there is an express provision to the contrary (Art. 39). The only relevant provision of the Anglo-Irish Agreement is the provision for review of the working of the Intergovernmental Conference under Article 11 at any time on the request of either party or in any event at the end of three years. As noted below, this provision does not include the review of the terms of Article 1 of the Agreement as to the status of Northern Ireland, which is to that extent "entrenched." But this does not exclude the general right of both parties to the Agreement to amend or modify any of its terms. The entrenched status of Article 1 does not therefore commit either party to an irrevocable position, provided the other party agrees to any proposed change. The consent of the people of Northern Ireland would not be required under international law except in so far as a right of self-determination might be held to arise, as discussed below.

Under the Vienna Convention a treaty may also be abandoned at any time with the consent of all the parties (Art. 54). The Vienna Convention further provides for the suspension of the operation of a treaty either in respect of a particular party or in respect of all parties if there is an express provision to that effect or if all parties after consultation agree (Art. 57). This is clearly a significant provision in the light of current discussions on possible means of securing greater involvement by unionists in Northern Ireland in the development or amendment of the Agreement.

Registration of a treaty with the United Nations does not affect these general rights of amendment, suspension or mutual abandonment. Registration is a separate duty imposed on all member states under the United Nations Charter (Art. 102) and is in theory, if not always in practice, a pre-condition of the invocation of the terms of the treaty before the International Court of Justice and other United Nations organs.

The status of the Agreement in national law

The challenges to the validity of the Agreement in both the British and the Irish courts have helped to clarify the status of the Agreement in national as well as in international law. Though the approach of the British and Irish courts in this respect has been similar, there are some significant differences.

(i) *Ex p. Molyneaux*

The challenge to the Agreement in the British courts in *Ex p. Molyneaux* [1986] 1 W. L. R. 331 was based on three separate grounds: that the establishment of the Intergovernmental Council was unlawful without legislation; that the Agreement fettered the statutory powers and duties of the Secretary of State for Northern Ireland; and that it infringed the Act of Union 1800 by denying to the Queen's subjects in Northern Ireland the same rights and privileges as her subjects in Great Britain. The application for leave to seek judicial review of the Agreement on the first of these grounds was firmly rejected in the initial *ex parte* hearing before Mann J. on November 20, 1985 and on all three grounds in the hearing in open court before Taylor J. on November 25, 1985. Taylor J. held that the fact that the Intergovernmental Council would have no legislative or executive power ruled out the need for any legislation to authorise it. He also held that the inclusion in Article 2(b) of the provision that "there is no derogation from the sovereignty of . . . the United Kingdom Government" and that it "retains responsibility for the decisions and administration of government within its own jurisdiction" clearly ruled out any argument that there was any fetter on the discretion of the Secretary of State. Finally, he rejected the argument based on Article 6 of the Act of Union, which provided that in any treaty with a foreign power subjects of the Crown in Ireland were to have the same privileges as those in Great Britain, on the ground that under the terms of section 2 of the Ireland Act 1949 the Republic of Ireland was not to be regarded as a foreign country and that consultation with the Government of the Republic on matters relating to Northern Ireland did not in any event place subjects of the Crown in Northern Ireland on any different footing than those in Great Britain who might also be affected by decisions of policy made with regard to Northern Ireland.

(ii) *McGimpsey & McGimpsey v. Ireland*
    The challenge to the validity of the Agreement in the Irish courts in *McGimpsey & McGimpsey* v. *Ireland* (unreported, High Court, July 29, 1988) was based on a number of alleged conflicts between the terms of the Agreement and the Irish Constitution. The principal argument was that the terms of Article 1 of the Agreement conflicted with the terms of Articles 2 and 3 of the Constitution. As explained in greater detail below in the note to Article 1, Barrington J. dismissed this argument on the ground that though Articles 2 and 3 could be treated alternatively as expressing a legal claim to Northern Ireland and as asserting merely a political claim, there was no conflict on either view since Article 1 of the Agreement merely expressed "a political judgment about likely future events." He also dismissed two further arguments similar to those raised in *Ex p. Molyneaux* [1986] 1 W.L.R. 331. In response to the argument that the Agreement fettered the discretion of the Irish Government, and therefore required specific constitutional authorisation in a similar way to that held to be required for the ratification of the Single European Act in *Crotty* v. *An Taoiseach* [1987] I.L.R.M. 400, the judge held that no such authorisation was required since the sovereignty of the Irish Government was expressly preserved in Article 2(c). And, in response to the argument that Article 5(c) of the Agreement was discriminatory in that it provided for the Irish Government to act on behalf of nationalists in Northern Ireland, thus excluding the interests of unionists, he held that the particular concern to eliminate discrimination against nationalists in Northern Ireland was not discriminatory and that the Agreement as a whole made it clear that the interests of both communities in Northern Ireland were to be respected. Finally, he rejected the argument that the Irish Government might in some way be estopped from pursuing its constitutional claim in Northern Ireland on the ground that it had not been shown that the making of the Agreement had in any way affected the position in international law of the respective claims of the United Kingdom and Ireland to Northern Ireland. He did, however, accept the right of the plaintiffs as unionists to institute proceedings for judicial review and declined to make an order for costs against them despite the failure of their action. An appeal against this judgment has been entered.
    In more general terms, it is clear from the judgments in these cases that both in British and Irish law the Agreement is regarded as having its effect

primarily in international law and that any challenge in national law must be to some specific legislative or administrative action under the Agreement. In *Ex p. Molyneaux* [1986] 1 W.L.R. 331 Taylor J. expressly stated that it was not the function of the court to interfere in the exercise of the royal prerogative in respect of the relations between the United Kingdom and another sovereign state (at p. 336). And in the *McGimpsey* case Barrington J. repeatedly stressed that the Agreement created obligations only in international law and that as such it was not open to challenge in the national courts unless and until some positive step was taken in national law to implement its provisions. The only major difference is that under Irish law the existence of a written constitution, and of some specific provision in Article 29 for certain matters in international law, makes it possible to raise a challenge to the validity of the Agreement over its effect in international law, notably in respect of any formal international acceptance of the status of Northern Ireland as part of the United Kingdom.

The political nature of the Agreement

The precise legal status of the Agreement or of particular provisions in it, whether in international or domestic law, may not always be of primary importance. For many purposes the Agreement may be considered as a political rather than a legal document. As will be seen, many of its provisions are drafted with the flexibility of politics rather than the precision of law in view. The real significance of the Agreement in this context is to establish new institutional arrangements and a new procedure for the two Governments to deal with the Northern Ireland problem. The value of these institutional arrangements, notably the permanent secretariat, is in this sense independent of the substantive provisions of the Agreement, which may be altered, developed or by-passed by those involved. The abandonment of any, or even all, of the substantive provisions agreed in 1985 would not therefore necessarily involve the abandonment of the new institutional arrangements. Those most closely involved with the Anglo-Irish Agreement emphasise its significance as a political process rather than as a legally binding agreement. The terms of the Agreement as it was entered into in 1985 nonetheless set some parameters for future political action and cannot be entirely ignored either by political representatives or by the officials who work it.

CHAPTER 2

ANNOTATION OF THE AGREEMENT

THE ANGLO-IRISH AGREEMENT 1985

Agreement between the Government of the United Kingdom of Great Britain and Northern Ireland and the Government of the Republic of Ireland (British version)

Agreement between the Government of Ireland and the Government of the United Kingdom (Irish version)

GENERAL NOTE

The use of differing terminology to describe the parties in treaties between the United Kingdom of Great Britain and Northern Ireland and Ireland and the signing of two separate versions is not new. It was said to be standard practice in a written answer to a Parliamentary Question on the point by Sir John Biggs-Davison: "In accordance with standard international practice, precedence is given to the United Kingdom in the original retained in London and to the Republic of Ireland in the original retained in Dublin. In addition, and in line with long established precedent in bilateral treaties with the Republic, each country's original of the agreement uses its own nomenclature in reference to itself and to the other country. There are no substantive differences between the texts, both originals of which are authoritative." (H.C. Deb. col. 132w (December 17, 1985)). Though this is true, practice has not been entirely uniform over the years. In the original treaty of 1921 both parties signed the same version referring to the parties as Great Britain and Ireland. In 1938 the trade war was ended by a treaty signed in two versions referring to the parties as the United Kingdom and Éire (British version) and the United Kingdom and Ireland (Irish version). In 1960 the Trade Agreement referred to the parties as the United Kingdom and the Republic of Ireland (British version) and Ireland and the United Kingdom (Irish version). In the same year, however, the British version of an Agreement on Social Security referred to the United Kingdom by its full title of the "United Kingdom of Great Britain and Northern Ireland." In multilateral treaties, however, both states have been willing to sign versions using the official names of both states, namely the United Kingdom of Great Britain and Northern Ireland and Ireland, as for instance in the Protocol for the prolongation of the International Sugar Agreement in 1966 and in the Treaty to extend the European Community in 1972.

The choice of differing descriptions for the two states in bilateral treaties and the resulting signature of different versions clearly reflects the underlying problem of conflicting claims over Northern Ireland. The terminology in the version of the Agreement signed by Mrs Thatcher uses the full title "the United Kingdom of Great Britain and Northern Ireland" which clearly asserts British jurisdiction over Northern Ireland; the use of the words "the Republic of Ireland" further emphasises the partition of Ireland. The use in the Irish version of the single word "Ireland" and the shortened title "the United Kingdom," omitting any reference to Northern Ireland, likewise reflects the unwillingness of the Irish Government to use words which might be taken to signify a formal acceptance that Northern Ireland is part of the United Kingdom. Mutual agreement to use the proper state names in all treaties, whether bilateral or multilateral, would be a distinct advance.

The Government of Ireland and the Government of the United Kingdom (Irish version)

The Government of the United Kingdom of Great Britain and Northern Ireland and the Government of the Republic of Ireland (British version)

Wishing further to develop the unique relationship between their peoples and the close co-operation between their countries as friendly neighbours and as partners in the European Community;

Recognising the major interest of both their countries and, above all, of the people of Northern Ireland in diminishing the divisions there and achieving lasting peace and stability;

Recognising the need for continuing efforts to reconcile and to acknowledge the rights of the two major traditions that exist in Ireland, represented on the one hand by those who wish for no change in the present status of Northern Ireland and on the other hand by those who aspire to a sovereign united Ireland achieved by peaceful means and through agreement;

Reaffirming their total rejection of any attempt to promote political objectives by violence or the threat of violence and their determination to work together to ensure that those who adopt or support such methods do not succeed;

Recognising that a condition of genuine reconciliation and dialogue between unionists and nationalists is mutual recognition and acceptance of each other's rights;

Recognising and respecting the identities of the two communities in Northern Ireland, and the right of each to pursue its aspirations by peaceful and constitutional means;

Reaffirming their commitment to a society in Northern Ireland in which all may live in peace, free from discrimination and intolerance, and with the opportunity for both communities to participate fully in the structures and processes of government;

Have accordingly agreed as follows:

GENERAL NOTE

The Preamble to the Agreement is an important statement of shared principles and objectives in approaching the Northern Ireland problem. It draws heavily on the wording used in the *New Ireland Forum Report*. It is expressly provided in the *Vienna Convention on the Law of Treaties* that a treaty is to be interpreted in accordance with the ordinary meaning to be given to its terms in their context, which in turn is expressly stated to include the preamble (Art. 31).

ANNOTATIONS

"The Government of Ireland, etc." See note above on the different versions of this.

"Unique relationship" This phrase was first officially used in the communique of the summit between Mrs Thatcher and Mr Haughey on May 21, 1980 (see above).

"Partners in the European Community" The fact that the European Community was initially formed as an association of previously warring countries which have now agreed to work together for mutual economic and social benefit provides a useful example for Britain and Ireland. The European Commission and other members of the Community have provided consistent support and encouragement for parallel developments between Britain and Ireland.

"Lasting peace and stability" This phrase was used in the terms of reference for the New Ireland Forum which was established "for consultations on the manner in which lasting peace and stability could be achieved in a new Ireland through the democratic process . . . " The phrase *"peace, reconciliation and stability"* was used in the communique of the summit meetings between Mrs Thatcher and Mr Haughey on December 8, 1980, and Mrs Thatcher and Dr Fitzgerald on November 7, 1983, and also in paragraph 4.15 of the *New Ireland Forum Report*.

"to reconcile and to acknowledge the rights of the two major traditions that exist in Ireland" This phrase is drawn from paragraph 4.16 of the *New Ireland Forum Report* and is central to the Irish view of the objectives of the Agreement. Explicit governmental recognition that there are two distinct traditions and communities in both Northern Ireland and Ireland as a whole and that something should be done to recognise and accommodate them—as opposed to assuming that any differences were negligible and to be ignored—was first made in the communique of the summit meeting between Mrs Thatcher and Dr Fitzgerald on November 6, 1981 in which reference was made to "the need for efforts to diminish the divisions between the two major sections of the community in Northern Ireland and to reconcile the two major traditions that exist in the two parts of Ireland." This theme was taken up in respect of Northern Ireland in the White Paper *A Framework for Devolution* published by the then Secretary of State for Northern Ireland, James Prior, in April 1982 (Cmnd. 8541, paras. 14 to 20). It

also formed a major part of the statement of "realities and requirements" in respect of Ireland as a whole in the *New Ireland Forum Report* published in May 1984 (paras. 5.2 and 5.3).

"represented on the one hand by those who wish for no change in the present status of Northern Ireland and on the other hand by those who aspire to a sovereign united Ireland" This description of the two traditions is based exclusively on differences in political aspiration as opposed to the religious and cultural differences which are associated with them. This formulation allows the two traditions to be referred to elsewhere in the Agreement as "unionist" and "nationalist" rather than "Protestant" and "Catholic" or "loyalist" and "republican," descriptions which are popularly used but which would have caused difficulties for the two Governments. In some instances, however, the two traditions in Northern Ireland are referred to as communities and the nationalist community is referred to as the minority community.

"a sovereign united Ireland achieved by peaceful means and through agreement" This phrase is a deliberate echo of paragraphs 5.4 and 5.7 of the *New Ireland Forum Report*. The formulation of the nationalist aspiration is restrictive in two ways: it asserts that the aspiration is exclusively for a sovereign united Ireland, and that those who seek to achieve unity by other means are to be excluded. The New Ireland Forum was constituted on a similar basis to include only those who sought to achieve "a New Ireland through the democratic process" and thus included representatives only of "democratic parties which reject violence," though it did not exclude other forms of unity or stability in a New Ireland. This restrictive definition of nationalism, colloquially referred to as "constitutional nationalism," is clearly intended to exclude those who seek to achieve a united Ireland by violence or coercion, notably Provisional Sinn Féin and the IRA. The difference between constitutional nationalism in this sense and nationalism which regards physical force or the armed struggle as legitimate was clarified in the papers produced by the Social Democratic and Labour Party and Provisional Sinn Féin during their abortive talks from March to September 1988 (*Irish Times*, September 12, 1988 at p. 11; September 13, 1988 at p. 8; September 19, 1988 at p. 10; September 26, 1988 at p. 10). It is questionable, given the large numbers who support or acquiesce in the use of violent means, whether it is factually correct to define the nationalist tradition in this way, though the reluctance of both Governments to give any credence to that part of the nationalist tradition is wholly understandable.

"reaffirming their total rejection of any attempt to promote political objectives by violence or the threat of violence" Though violence has been rejected by the two Governments in successive summits this particular formulation was first used in the communique of the summit meeting between Mrs Thatcher and Dr Fitzgerald on November 18–19, 1984. It reflects the definition of "terrorism" in both the Prevention of Terrorism (Temporary Provisions) Acts 1974, 1976 and 1984 and the Northern Ireland (Emergency Provisions) Acts 1973 and 1978 as "the use of violence for political ends . . . "

"their determination to work together to ensure that those who adopt or support such methods do not succeed" This is a significant extension of the standard and at times almost ritual condemnation of violence. Though both Governments have acted firmly within their own jurisdictions against the IRA, the Agreement commits them to co-operation in both jurisdictions against all forms of political violence.

"a condition of genuine reconciliation and dialogue between unionists and nationalists is mutual recognition and acceptance of each other's rights" The general concept of mutual respect by nationalists and unionists of each other's rights was first made explicit in the communique of the summit meeting between Mrs Thatcher and Dr Fitzgerald on November 6, 1981. It was central to the "rolling devolution" proposals in April 1982 (Cmnd. 8541). It also reflects the formulation in paragraph 4.15 of the *New Ireland Forum Report*. Though the precise extent of those rights is not spelled out, certain aspects in relation to self-determination by the people of Northern Ireland and the rights of the nationalist minority within Northern Ireland are further clarified in subsequent provisions.

"recognising and respecting the identities of the two communities in Northern Ireland" Here, and in most other provisions, the drafters chose to refer to the existence of two separate *communities* in Northern Ireland, as opposed to the existence of two *traditions* in Ireland as a whole (see above). The word "tradition" does not imply the same close and often exclusive relationships as "community". The use of the words "respecting the identities" may be traced most directly to the *New Ireland Forum Report*, e.g. para. 5.2., and to the communique of the summit meeting between Mrs Thatcher and Dr Fitzgerald on November 18–19, 1984. The specific measures for this purpose are set out in Article 5.

"the right of each to pursue its aspirations by peaceful and constitutional means" The explicit recognition of the right of each community to pursue its aspirations played a larger part in the

documents leading up to the Sunningdale Conference and communique in 1973 than in the period from 1981 to 1985. However, no specific provisions were made in the Northern Ireland Constitution Act 1973 or in the Anglo-Irish Agreement to give effect to this right, presumably on the grounds that it was not thought to be necessary. The argument that formal constitutional provisions in respect of aspirations might be desirable is discussed below in the commentary on Article 1.

"reaffirming their commitment" The previous commitments by the two Governments were somewhat less specific: in the communique of the summit meeting between Mrs Thatcher and Dr Fitzgerald on November 18–19, 1984 it was agreed that "the identities of both the majority and the minority communities in Northern Ireland should be recognised and respected and reflected in the structures and processes of Northern Ireland in ways acceptable to both communities," and that "the process of government in Northern Ireland should be such as to provide the people of both communities with the confidence that their rights will be safeguarded"; see also para. 4.15 of the *New Ireland Forum Report*.

"a society in Northern Ireland in which all may live in peace, free from discrimination and intolerance" This formulation is much more general and positive than previous declarations on this matter by either Government. The participants in the New Ireland Forum committed themselves to "new structures in which no tradition will be allowed to dominate the other, in which there will be provision for formal and effective guarantees for the protection of individual human rights and of the communal and cultural rights of both nationalists and unionists;" they also agreed that "civil and religious liberties and rights must be guaranteed and there can be no discrimination or preference in laws or administrative practices, on grounds of religious belief or persuasion" (paras. 5.2(5) and 5.2(6)). But these protections were envisaged for a new Ireland rather than for Northern Ireland alone. The British Government had committed itself to the prevention of religious and political discrimination by law or by public administration both under the Government of Ireland Act 1920 (s.5) and under the Northern Ireland Constitution Act 1973 (ss.17 to 19). But protection from discrimination in the private sector is more limited and there are no provisions on intolerance. The specific provisions of the Agreement on these matters are included in Article 5(a).

"with the opportunity for both communities to participate fully in the structures and processes of government" The British Government has been committed since the introduction of direct rule in 1972 to a form of devolved government in Northern Ireland "which is likely to be widely accepted throughout the community" as provided in the Northern Ireland Constitution Act 1973 (s.2). The focus of the New Ireland Forum on new structures for the whole of Ireland did not permit any explicit statement on the form of government within Northern Ireland as such. The specific provisions of the Agreement on these matters are set out in Article 4.

A: STATUS OF NORTHERN IRELAND

Article 1

The two Governments
- (a) affirm that any change in the status of Northern Ireland would only come about with the consent of a majority of the people of Northern Ireland;
- (b) recognise that the present wish of a majority of the people of Northern Ireland is for no change in the status of Northern Ireland;
- (c) declare that, if in the future a majority of the people of Northern Ireland clearly wish for and formally consent to the establishment of a united Ireland, they will introduce and support in the respective Parliaments legislation to give effect to that wish.

GENERAL NOTE

In the drafting of this Article there was a conscious effort by both sides to avoid dispute on the definition of a current status for Northern Ireland. As was said at the time the two states came to the negotiations with "different title deeds". As a result the emphasis in Article 1 is laid on the agreed conditions for any future change in the status of Northern Ireland. The intention was to reassure unionists that their right to remain in the United Kingdom, as declared in section 1 of the Northern Ireland Constitution Act 1973, was formally recognised by the Irish Government, while at the same time assuring nationalists that if they secured the consent of unionists for a united Ireland the British Government would implement it. This joint purpose was to be further emphasised by excluding the Article from the review process under Article 11. But it is questionable whether any of these purposes was satisfactorily achieved.

In the first place, the concern of those who drafted the Article to avoid any potential conflict with Articles 2 and 3 of the Irish Constitution resulted in a weaker rather than a stronger form of guarantee for unionists. In the initial negotiations on the Agreement there was some discussion of changing Articles 2 and 3 of the Irish Constitution in the context of a more radical reassessment of the arrangements for governing Northern Ireland. But the British side considered that the price demanded by the Irish for this concession was too high. As a result it was decided that the Agreement would have to be drafted to give as strong a guarantee to unionists as was consistent with the constitutional claim in Articles 2 and 3 of the Irish Constitution.

Two significant changes were made compared with the terms of the Sunningdale communique (see above): the declaration was a joint one by both Governments as opposed to the separate and parallel declarations made at Sunningdale; and the word "would" was substituted for "could" in relation to any change in the status of Northern Ireland. The result of the former change was that no declaration at all was made as to what the status of Northern Ireland is, even by the British Government which at Sunningdale had clearly declared that it was part of the United Kingdom. The result of the latter was that the declaration ceased on one view to have any possible legal as opposed to factual significance. This view was neatly summarised by Barrington J. in *McGimpsey & McGimpsey* v. *Ireland* (unreported, High Court, July 29, 1988): "It appears to me that in Article 1 of the Agreement the two Governments merely recognise the situation on the ground in Northern Ireland (paragraph (*b*)), form a political judgment about the likely course of future events (paragraph (*a*)), and state what their policy will be should events evolve in a particular way (paragraph (*c*))." For a different view of the effect of paragraph (*c*) see below.

The fear of possible constitutional challenge to the Agreement on the part of those concerned in drafting it clearly stemmed from the previous experience of the two Governments over the Sunningdale declarations. Though the constitutional challenge in that case was not successful in legal as opposed to political terms, the Irish Supreme Court had left open the possibility that some more formal recognition by the Irish Government of the status of Northern Ireland as part of the United Kingdom might be unconstitutional (see above). The terms of Articles 2 and 3 are as follows:

2. The national territory consists of the whole island of Ireland, its islands and the territorial seas.

3. Pending the re-integration of the national territory, and without prejudice to the right of the Parliament and Government established by this Constitution to exercise jurisdiction over the whole of that territory, the laws exacted by that Parliament shall have the like area and extent of operation as the laws of Saorstát Éireann and the like extra-territorial effect.

Two broad views have emerged in recent cases on the meaning and effect of these confusing and apparently contradictory provisions. The first and intuitively more acceptable view is that they were intended to and do assert a formal constitutional claim over the whole of Ireland while at the same time stating that for practical legal purposes jurisdiction will only be exercised over the twenty-six counties which constituted the Irish Free State (Saorstát Éireann) from 1921 until the adoption of the new Irish Constitution in 1937. This view is popularly accepted both by republicans and by unionists, and is a continuing issue of contention between them. It was adopted by counsel on *both* sides in *McGimpsey & McGimpsey* v. *Ireland* (unreported, High Court, July 29, 1988), presumably because it offered the best chance of success to the challengers and because it would have been politically difficult for a Fianna Fáil government to adopt any other view. The judges in the Irish courts, however, have recently favoured a second view, that the Articles express a claim only in the realm of political theory. This view was most directly expressed by O'Higgins C.J. in a reference as to the constitutionality of the Criminal Law Jurisdiction Bill: he stated that the Constitution contained not only legal rules but expressed the political theories about the rights of nations as opposed to states held by those who drafted it and that the "national claim to unity exists not in the legal but in the political order" (*Re Article 26 and the Criminal Law (Jurisdiction) Bill 1975* [1977] I.R. 129, at p. 147). It was also explained at some length in the judgment of Barrington J. in *McGimpsey & McGimpsey* v. *Ireland* (unreported, High Court, July 29, 1988), though on the interpretation which he adopted of Article 1 of the Agreement it was not necessary for him to decide between it and the view put to him by counsel on both sides. The form of the wording in Article 1, notably the use of "would" for "could" and the careful avoidance of any explicit statement as to what the constitutional status of Northern Ireland is, however, suggests that the two Governments took the view that Articles 2 and 3 of the Irish Constitution could be interpreted as asserting a legal claim over Northern Ireland, and that any resulting constitutional challenge to the Agreement was to be avoided at all costs. Article 1 may thus be viewed as expressing the best guarantee to unionists that was compatible with the stronger interpretation of Articles 2 and 3 of the Irish Constitution. Since it is precisely the continuing presence of the claim in Articles 2 and 3 that is of concern to unionists it is hardly surprising that few unionists were impressed by the argument that Article 1 represented a new and stronger recognition by Ireland of the status of Northern Ireland.

In the second place the exclusion of Article 1 from the review procedure provided for in Article 11 gives little if any additional guarantee that the declarations by the two Governments will not be altered. As explained in the general introductory note on the status of the Agreement, in international law any provision of a bilateral treaty may at any time be altered, suspended or abandoned with the consent of both parties. As a guarantee to unionists, who were not and in international law perhaps could not have been a party to the Agreement as a treaty, the Agreement is therefore less than convincing since the British and Irish Governments might at any time agree to alter or abandon the principle of consent as it is expressed in Article 1. Though the Irish Government may perhaps be regarded as a satisfactory long-term guarantor for nationalists in Northern Ireland, the British Government is not generally regarded as sufficiently committed to the interests of unionists to be a satisfactory long-term guarantor for them.

One possible approach to resolving this difficulty in providing a satisfactory long-term guarantee on the status of Northern Ireland would be to include as a party to a future agreement or treaty a representative or guarantor of the unionist as opposed to the general British interest. The absence of an elected government of Northern Ireland, however, and the fact that any such government would not be an independent state party would make this difficult to achieve. The involvement in a treaty of an independent body such as the European Commission might prove a better protection against a decision by future British and Irish Governments to abandon any guarantee.

A more generally satisfactory solution, as argued below, may be to define and entrench, in so far as that is possible, the status of Northern Ireland in the internal constitutional law both of Ireland and of the United Kingdom. It has already been proposed on a number of occasions that Articles 2 and 3 of the Irish Constitution should be amended to express an aspiration for eventual unification by consent rather than a claim, whether in the legal or the political realm. An all-party committee of Dáil Éireann established in 1966 to review the Irish Constitution recommended that Article 3 should be reformulated to express such an aspiration in the following words:

> The Irish nation hereby proclaims its firm will that its territory be reunited in harmony and brotherly affection between all Irishmen.
>
> The laws enacted by the Parliament established by this Constitution shall, until the achievement of the nation's unity shall otherwise require, have the like area and extent of application as the laws of the Parliament which existed prior to the adoption of this Constitution. Provision may be made by law to give extra-territorial effect to such laws. (Pr. 9817)

But this would have left intact the claim in Article 2 that the national territory extended over the whole island of Ireland. The revised version proposed by the Progressive Democrats in January 1988 was as follows:

> The people of Ireland hereby proclaim their firm will that the national territory, which consists of the whole island of Ireland, its islands and territorial seas, be reunited in harmony and by consent.
>
> The laws enacted by the Parliament established by this Constitution shall, until the achievement of the nation's unity shall otherwise require, have the like area and extent of application as the laws of the Parliament which existed prior to the adoption of this Constitution. Provision may be made by law to give extra-territorial effect to such laws.

Whether a reformulation of this kind would be sufficient to remove finally the conflicting claims, whether legal or political, which have bedevilled relations between the two parts of Ireland must be doubtful. It would be preferable, if it could be achieved, for the current status of Northern Ireland as part of the United Kingdom and the aspiration of some of its people and of the people of Ireland to be set down in the same words both in the Irish Constitution and a new Northern Ireland Constitution Act.

ANNOTATIONS

"*The two Governments*" The use of this form of words permitted the wording of the substance of the Agreement to be identical in the two versions signed by the two sides.

"*affirm*" The use of this word, rather than "fully accepted and solemnly declared" as in the Sunningdale communiqué (see above), was considered by Barrington J. in the *McGimpsey* case (above), to lessen the force of the commitment in political if not in legal terms. Both words are used in section 1 of the Northern Ireland Constitution Act 1973 which states that "it is hereby declared that Northern Ireland remains part of Her Majesty's dominions and of the United Kingdom, and it is hereby affirmed that in no event will Northern Ireland or any part of it cease to be part of Her Majesty's dominions and of the United Kingdom without the consent of the majority of the people of Northern Ireland voting in a poll . . . "

"that any change in the status of Northern Ireland would only come about" The use of the word "would," rather than "could" as in the equivalent part of the Sunningdale communique, may be traced back to the communique of the summit meeting between Mr. Haughey and Mrs Thatcher on May 21, 1980 and appears to have been intended to turn what might have been a legal commitment into a factual statement, thus avoiding any potential constitutional challenge: see the judgment of Barrington J. in *McGimpsey & McGimpsey* v. *Ireland* (above). There is no statement by either Government as to what the status of Northern Ireland is; in the Sunningdale communique the British Government, though not the Irish Government, stated that it was part of the United Kingdom.

"with the consent of a majority of the people of Northern Ireland" This formulation may also be traced back to the communique of the summit on May 21, 1980. The consent of a majority of the people presumably means the consent of a simple majority of those voting in a referendum as provided for in the "border poll" provisions of the Northern Ireland Constitution Act 1973 (s.1 and Sched. 1). It would also be possible to argue that a given proportion of those entitled to vote as opposed to those actually voting should be required, as for example in the provisions for a 40 per cent. minimum for the referendum on devolution to Scotland and Wales under the Scotland and Wales Act 1978. In the *New Ireland Forum Report* all the participating parties agreed that "the political arrangements for a new and sovereign Ireland would have to be freely negotiated and agreed to by the people of the North and the people of the South" (para. 5.2(3)). There was no discussion of precisely how this agreement was to be assessed, but the implication is that separate referendums would be required in Northern Ireland and the rest of Ireland.

"recognise that the present wish of a majority of the people of Northern Ireland is for no change in the status of Northern Ireland" From an Irish viewpoint this recognition may be seen as a significant concession. In the last official "border poll" in March 1973, 591,820 (58 per cent.) of the voting population in Northern Ireland voted to stay in the United Kingdom, 6,463 (1 per cent.) voted for a united Ireland and the rest abstained. Successive opinion polls have confirmed that a clear majority of voters in Northern Ireland wish to remain in the United Kingdom. As in the case of paragraph (a) the joint recognition of this fact would not appear to have any legal effect: see the judgment of Barrington J. in *McGimpsey & McGimpsey* v. *Ireland* (above).

"declare that" It would appear, contrary to the view expressed by Barrington J. in *McGimpsey & McGimpsey* v. *Ireland* (above), that this paragraph does constitute an undertaking which is binding in international law rather than a mere statement of fact or policy. On this view, the sole legal effect of Article 1 is to impose a binding international commitment on the British Government to legislate for a united Ireland if a majority in Northern Ireland so wish.

"if in the future a majority of the people of Northern Ireland clearly wish for and formally consent to" This formulation envisages a two-stage process: first, the clear expression of a wish, perhaps in the form of an agreement between political leaders or the results of a credible opinion poll, and then, a formal expression of majority consent, presumably in a "border poll" of the kind provided for under the Northern Ireland Constitution Act (see above). It is again unclear whether a simple majority of those voting or a simple majority of those entitled to vote is required.

"the establishment of a united Ireland" The precise form of united Ireland is not clarified. The *New Ireland Forum Report* identified two major possibilities: a unitary state and a federal or confederal state. It is clear that the people of Northern Ireland are *not* being offered unfettered self-determination of the kind envisaged under the United Nations Charter and Covenants, in that no other status than that of being part of the United Kingdom or part of a united Ireland is provided for. Independence or even a condominium between Britain and Ireland of the kind also discussed in the *New Ireland Forum Report* are not provided for under the Agreement, though that does not of course rule them out since both Governments may subsequently decide to abandon the Agreement and seek other solutions. There is no clear definition of a "people" for the purposes of the exercise of a right to full self-determination under the United Nations Charter and Covenants. It is generally thought that the existence of a well-defined territory populated by a coherent ethnic or cultural group is required but that there is no general right of secession for a minority within an established state even if it is concentrated in a particular region or part of that state: for a full discussion of these issues see *The Report of the Special Rapporteur on the Right to Self-determination: Historical and Current*

Developments (Critescu Report), United Nations 1981 and *The Report of the Special Rapporteur on the Right to Self-determination: Implementation of United Nations Resolutions* (Espiell Report), United Nations 1981.

"*they will introduce and support in the respective Parliaments*" These words are used to avoid any implication that it is the Governments as opposed to their respective Parliaments that have control over legislation; the addition of the word 'support' is presumably intended to prevent either government from taking a neutral stance on such legislation. This is a somewhat stronger form of undertaking by the British Government than in the Sunningdale communique which merely stated that if a majority of the people in Northern Ireland should in the future indicate a wish to become part of a united Ireland the British Government would support that wish. This undertaking has been taken by some nationalists, notably the Social Democratic and Labour Party in Northern Ireland, as a significant declaration by the British Government that it has no long-term interest in the maintenance of the union between Great Britain and Northern Ireland.

"*legislation to give effect to that wish*" British practice on the grant of independence to former colonial territories has been to enact legislation at Westminster to establish a new constitution for the emerging state. Whether this would be necessary in the event of agreement on a new constitution for Ireland is doubtful. But there would certainly be a need for British legislation to recognise the new status of Northern Ireland and for financial and administrative matters. There is no undertaking by the British Government to provide any financial support for a newly united Ireland to replace the substantial support currently given to Northern Ireland within the United Kingdom.

B: THE INTERGOVERNMENTAL CONFERENCE

Article 2

(*a*) There is hereby established, within the framework of the Anglo-Irish Intergovernmental Council set up after the meeting between the two Heads of Government on 6 November 1981, an Intergovernmental Conference (hereinafter referred to as 'the Conference') concerned with Northern Ireland and with relations between the two parts of the island of Ireland, to deal, as set out in this Agreement, on a regular basis with
(i) political matters;
(ii) security and related matters;
(iii) legal matters, including the administration of justice;
(iv) the promotion of cross-border co-operation.
(*b*) The United Kingdom Government accept that the Irish Government will put forward views and proposals on matters relating to Northern Ireland within the field of activity of the Conference in so far as those matters are not the responsibility of a devolved administration in Northern Ireland. In the interests of promoting peace and stability, determined efforts shall be made through the Conference to resolve any differences. The Conference will be mainly concerned with Northern Ireland; but some of the matters under consideration will involve co-operative action in both parts of Ireland, and possibly also in Great Britain. Some of the proposals considered in respect of Northern Ireland may also be found to have application by the Irish Government. There is no derogation from the sovereignty of either the United Kingdom Government or the Irish Government, and each retains responsibility for the decisions and administration of government within its own jurisdiction.
[This is the British version; in the Irish version precedence is given to the Irish Government.]

GENERAL NOTE

The Intergovernmental Conference is the centre-piece of the Agreement. In formal terms it is a development of and operates within the framework of the Anglo-Irish Intergovernmental Council established in 1981 to provide a co-ordinated structure for all dealings between the

British and Irish Governments at both ministerial and official levels. But its role and functions are much more specifically defined.

The primary function of the Conference is to provide a forum for discussion between the two Governments on certain matters relating to the internal affairs of Northern Ireland, notably the protection of the interests of the nationalist minority and certain related security and legal matters, and more generally on matters involving cross-border co-operation between the two parts of Ireland. But it is made clear that if agreement on a form of devolved government in Northern Ireland which is acceptable to both communities can be reached the Conference will cease to have any function in respect of matters on which responsibility is devolved. In addition the Conference is granted authority to concern itself with some matters, other than cross-border co-operation, which relate to the internal government of Ireland and possibly even Great Britain, though these are not specified in any detail. This reflects a clear hierarchy in the concerns of the Conference: firstly, Northern Ireland affairs; secondly, matters involving co-operation by the Irish or British Governments; and finally, matters on which action in Northern Ireland might be followed by the Irish Government in its own jurisdiction. The overall structure for intergovernmental relations may thus be portrayed in simplified form as follows:

Anglo-Irish Intergovernmental Council
Matters of general concern to the United Kingdom and Ireland such as trade and cultural relations (the east-west dimension)

Anglo-Irish Intergovernmental Conference
Matters within Northern Ireland, particularly those which involve the interests of the minority nationalist community, except in so far as they are devolved to an administration in which representatives of that community are directly involved (the internal Northern Ireland dimension)

Matters of particular concern to both parts of Ireland such as co-operation in cross-border security and the promotion of cross-border economic, social and cultural co-operation (the north-south dimension)

As will be seen, however, the demarcation lines are not always drawn as clearly as this simple summary suggests and there is a general lack of clarity on the extent to which reciprocal action to that discussed in relation to Northern Ireland can be proposed for Ireland or Great Britain.

The mode of operation of the Conference, unlike that of the Council, is also specified in some detail. It is expressly stated that the Irish Government may put forward "views and proposals" in relation to the internal Northern Ireland dimension, in so far as the relevant matters have not been devolved, and that "determined efforts shall be made . . . to resolve any differences." It is implied, though not stated, that a similar arrangement applies in relation to proposals for cross-border co-operation or reciprocal action by either side. But sovereignty and exclusive responsibility for decision-making within its own jurisdiction is expressly reserved on both sides. There is express provision for meetings at both official and ministerial level and also for the attendance of professional advisers, such as the Chief Constable of the Royal Ulster Constabulary and the Commissioner of the Garda Síochána. There is also express provision for the establishment of a Secretariat on a continuing basis, though not for its location.

This arrangement clearly falls far short of any form of joint authority over Northern Ireland. The obligation to make determined efforts to resolve any differences has been said to make the working of the Conference "more than consultative" though "less than executive." Joint authority of the kind envisaged in the *New Ireland Forum Report* (Chap. 8) and in the *Kilbrandon Committee Report* would require not only the explicit sharing of responsibility for decision-making but also almost inevitably some sharing of responsibility for the finances of Northern Ireland as a separate unit. In the *Forum Report* study on possible forms of joint authority it was envisaged that Britain and Ireland would contribute in proportion to their respective gross national products (*The Macroeconomic Consequences of Integrated Economic Policy, Planning and Co-ordination in Ireland*). On this basis the contribution by Ireland to any deficit in the finances of Northern Ireland under joint authority would have been of the order of 5 per cent. on 1983 figures (*ibid.*, p. 21). Whether on this basis Ireland could have expected to have an equal say in decision-making is at least debatable. Another possibility would be to allocate financial responsibility on the basis of the ratio between the unionist and nationalist communities in Northern Ireland, *i.e.* approximately 60 : 40. The model for joint authority proposed by the *Kilbrandon Report* adopted a similar approach to the allocation of decision-making power in that the ruling executive would have been composed of one British Government representative, one Irish Government representative, and two unionist and one nationalist representative elected within Northern Ireland; with simple majority voting on the executive this would have prevented either unionists or nationalists from imposing their will without the support of the British or Irish Government representatives (paras. 12.10 to 12.18). There would be similar problems under any form of joint authority in the allocation of powers to legislate for and raise taxes in Northern Ireland, and in the relationship between the powers of the British and Irish Governments and any locally elected Northern Ireland Assembly. It would be possible under the terms of the current Agreement for the British Government to permit the Irish Government to have greater *de facto* influence over administrative decision-making in Northern Ireland. But any move towards the formal recognition of any system of joint authority would clearly require major changes not only in the terms of the Agreement but also in the legislative and financial arrangements for Northern Ireland.

ANNOTATIONS

"There is hereby established" There is no other formal provision for the Conference either in legislation or otherwise in either the United Kingdom or Ireland. Though the Conference could not be unilaterally disestablished without a breach of international law, its existence and operation is regarded under British law as an exercise of the royal prerogative in respect of relations between the United Kingdom and another sovereign state (see *Ex p. Molyneaux* [1986] 1 W.L.R. 331, at p. 336, *per* Taylor J.) and under Irish law as an exercise of the executive power of the state in connection with its external relations under Article 28 of the Irish Constitution (*McGimpsey & McGimpsey* v. *Ireland* (unreported, High Court, July 29, 1988) *per* Barrington J.).

"within the framework of the Anglo-Irish Intergovernmental Council set up after the meeting between the two Heads of Government on 6 November 1981" As explained in the general introductory note above, the Anglo-Irish Intergovernmental Council is little more than a name for the continuing series of intergovernmental contacts at ministerial and official levels. Like the Conference it has no formal legislative foundation. Unlike the Conference it has no officially designated secretariat; business within its framework is organised by an informal steering group of senior officials.

"an Intergovernmental Conference (hereinafter referred to as 'the Conference')" The choice of the word "conference" seems to have been determined partly by the need to distinguish it from the Council and partly by the desire to emphasise that it did not have a decision-making role.

"concerned with Northern Ireland and with relations between the two parts of the island of Ireland" This sets out the primary functions of the Conference, though reference is made in sub-article (b) to possible action in the Irish state or in Great Britain.

"to deal, as set out in this Agreement" This provision appears to limit the jurisdiction of the Conference to the matters specifically referred to in Articles 5 to 10.

"on a regular basis" There is a separate provision under Article 3 for "regular and frequent" ministerial meetings.

"(i) political matters" See Articles 5 and 6 below.

"(ii) security and related matters" See Article 7 below.

"(iii) legal matters, including the administration of justice" See Article 8 below.

"(iv) the promotion of cross-border co-operation" See Articles 9 and 10 below.

"The United Kingdom Government accept that the Irish Government will put forward views and proposals" This provides the essential basis for the Irish Government to become involved in matters which would otherwise be the exclusive and internal concern of the United Kingdom Government. There is no reciprocal provision for the United Kingdom Government to put forward views and proposals in relation to action by the Irish Government, though that has regularly been done. The choice of the words "views and proposals" seems to have been intended to emphasise that the Irish Government is entitled to express its views on relevant matters and to put forward its own proposals for action but not to be involved in the final decision-making process, which is reserved for the relevant ministers of the Northern Ireland Office and ultimately the British Cabinet.

"on matters relating to Northern Ireland within the field of activity of the Conference" This clearly limits the right of the Irish Government to put forward views and proposals on other matters, for example, in relation to the administration of justice in Britain. The proper forum for any such representations would be the Anglo-Irish Intergovernmental Council.

"in so far as those matters are not the responsibility of a devolved administration in Northern Ireland" This is an important provision which is designed to limit the jurisdiction of the Conference to matters for which responsibility has not been devolved to a Northern Ireland administration in accordance with Article 4(b). It was intended to act as an incentive to both unionists and nationalists within Northern Ireland to agree to some form of devolution so that they might take over responsibility for devolved matters and in so doing reduce the jurisdiction of the Conference. This is in accord with the general strategy embodied in the Agree-

ment, namely that the Irish Government should represent the interests of the nationalist minority in Northern Ireland until its own elected representatives had been enabled to do so themselves within a devolved administration. A similar provision is made in respect of cross-border co-operation under Article 10(b). There would nonetheless be likely to be some matters in respect of which the Conference would continue to have jurisdiction even if agreement were reached on a structure for devolution. The current provisions for devolution under the Northern Ireland Constitution Act 1973, as amended by the Northern Ireland Act 1982, provide for three categories of powers: (i) "transferred matters" for which responsibility was actually transferred in 1973 by a devolution order under section 2 of that Act; (ii) "reserved matters" for which responsibility might also be transferred by an order under section 3 of that Act, but for which it was not thought appropriate to make an initial devolution order in 1973; and (iii) "excepted matters" for which it was thought in 1973 that responsibility should never be devolved. "Excepted matters" are listed in Schedule 2 to the 1973 Act, and cover such matters as the Crown, international relations, the armed forces, taxation, the appointment of the judiciary and the Director of Public Prosecution, elections, and special powers for dealing with terrorism or subversion; "reserved matters" are listed in Schedule 3 to that Act and cover such matters as the courts, the police, the criminal law, relations with (the Republic of) Ireland, broadcasting and telecommunications, trade marks, and civil defence. Though this framework and these lists could at any time be altered by legislation at Westminster, it is clear that while they remain in force there would be a number of matters over which the Conference would retain jurisdiction even after the establishment of a devolved administration, notably both reserved and excepted matters to do with the administration of justice and emergency powers in respect of terrorism and subversion. If agreement were reached on the devolution of *all* matters over which the Conference has jurisdiction under the Agreement, the Conference would presumably cease to meet and its Secretariat would presumably be disbanded, leaving relations between the United Kingdom and Ireland on other matters to be dealt with under the Anglo-Irish Intergovernmental Council.

"*In the interests of promoting peace and stability*" This phrase echoes the sentiments in the third paragraph in the Preamble, but does not appear to have any operative effect in this Article other than to emphasise that the failure to achieve agreement is likely to hinder the achievement of peace and stability.

"*determined efforts shall be made through the Conference to resolve any differences*" This provision was intended to indicate that the function of the Conference was to be more than merely consultative though, as provided in the final sentence of Article 2(b), it was not a decision-making body. The words used should be read in the context of the joint commitment in the Preamble to work together for certain basic objectives. It is well established in the field of industrial relations that an obligation under an agreement to negotiate in good faith is more demanding than an obligation to inform or to consult. In practice the search for consensus is left to the Conference Secretariat, which is composed of civil servants from both states.

"*The Conference will be mainly concerned with Northern Ireland*" This provision emphasises that the primary function of the Conference is in respect of the internal dimension. The use of the word 'will' rather than 'shall' might on a strict legal construction be taken to turn this provision into a prediction rather than an obligation; it is more probable that it reflects the political rather than the legal approach of those who drafted the Agreement.

"*but some of the matters under consideration will involve co-operative action in both parts of the island of Ireland*" The primary application of this provision would appear to be in respect of cross-border co-operation under Articles 9 and 10; as with the foregoing provision it is drafted in a descriptive rather than a prescriptive manner.

"*and possibly also in Great Britain*" It is not clear what this tentative provision refers to. It may have been thought that some forms of co-operative action in the two parts of Ireland might require similar or reciprocal action in Great Britain, though no such action would appear to have been raised at Conference meetings to date. If the broad structure of the Agreement is followed, it should not apply to matters of concern to Great Britain and Ireland on an "east-west" basis, which would be within the jurisdiction of the Anglo-Irish Intergovernmental Council. For example, it appears that the Conference does not cover the discussion of issues arising out of the Birmingham Bombs trial though they were discussed directly between the Irish Minister for Foreign Affairs and the British Home Secretary.

"*Some of the proposals considered in respect of Northern Ireland may also be found to have application by the Irish Government*" This similarly tentative provision would appear to refer to possible reciprocal action by the Irish Government parallel to action by the British Government in Northern Ireland rather than to co-operative action of a cross-border character under Articles 9 and 10. For example, the discussion of a possible Bill of Rights for Northern Ireland led to a proposal for a joint declaration of rights by both Governments at the Conference meeting on October 6, 1986. Possible reciprocal action of this kind, however, has not figured prominently in the work of the Conference and the provision may be thought to have been inserted more for the appearance of reciprocity than with any intention that pressure should be exerted through the Conference for action to deal with such matters as the rights of the Protestant minority in Ireland.

"There is no derogation from the sovereignty of either the United Kingdom Government or the Irish Government" This provision appears to have been insisted on by the British side during negotiation of the Agreement. It played a significant role in the decision of the British and Irish courts in challenges to the Agreement in *Ex p. Molyneaux* [1986] 1 W.L.R. 331 and in *McGimpsey & McGimpsey* v. *Ireland*, (unreported, High Court, July 29, 1988) (see above).

"and each retains responsibility for the decisions and administration of government within its own jurisdiction" This provision spells out the practical implications of the retention of sovereignty by the two Governments. It clearly rules out any form of formal joint authority, as discussed in the general note above. But, as in the case of Article 1, the provision is carefully drafted to avoid any clear or exclusive statement as to what the jurisdiction of each Government might be.

Article 3

The Conference shall meet at Ministerial or official level, as required. The business of the Conference will thus receive attention at the highest level. Regular and frequent Ministerial meetings shall be held; and in particular special meetings shall be convened at the request of either side. Officials may meet in subordinate groups. Membership of the Conference and of sub-groups shall be small and flexible. When the Conference meets at Ministerial level an Irish Minister designated as the Permanent Irish Ministerial Representative and the Secretary of State for Northern Ireland shall be joint Chairmen. Within the framework of the Conference other Irish and British Ministers may hold or attend meetings as appropriate: when legal matters are under consideration the Attorneys General may attend. Ministers may be accompanied by their officials and their professional advisers: for example, when questions of security policy or security co-operation are being discussed, they may be accompanied by the Commissioner of the Garda Síochána and the Chief Constable of the Royal Ulster Constabulary; or when questions of economic or social policy or co-operation are being discussed, they may be accompanied by officials of the relevant Departments. A Secretariat shall be established by the two Governments to service the Conference on a continuing basis in the discharge of its functions as set out in this Agreement.

[This is the Irish version; in the British version precedence is given to British ministers and officials.]

ANNOTATIONS

"The Conference shall meet at Ministerial or official level, as required" As with the Anglo-Irish Intergovernmental Council, the Conference is taken to cover *all* meetings between representatives of the two Governments, whether between ministers or officials. In contrast to the Council, however, no attempt has been made to report the number of non-ministerial Conference meetings, perhaps because the existence of a permanent secretariat makes it difficult to do so.

"The business of the Conference will thus receive attention at the highest level" This sentence does not fit naturally in its present position. It appears to reflect an earlier draft which envisaged meetings of the Conference at the level of Heads of Government.

"Regular and frequent Ministerial meetings shall be held" This provision imposes a general obligation on both sides to give *ministerial* attention to the business of the Conference at regular and frequent intervals. To date it has been interpreted as permitting intervals of as little as two or three weeks and as much as four months between meetings. In the period from November 1985 until October 1988 a total of 25 meetings were held, *i.e.* an average of one every six weeks. The longest interval to date has been between the meetings of December 8, 1986 and April 6, 1987 when "talks about talks" were being held between the unionist leaders, Mr Molyneaux and Dr Paisley, and the Secretary of State for Northern Ireland and his officials.

"and in particular special meetings shall be convened at the request of either side" This provision allows either side to ensure that its interpretation of "regular and frequent" prevails. To

date five special meetings have been arranged, on December 30, 1985, July 29, 1986, October 31, 1986, November 16, 1987 and February 2, 1988, of which all but one were at the express request of the Irish side. The practice has been for such meetings to be restricted to particular issues of concern, *e.g.* a hunger strike in December 1985, the security implications of the Enniskillen bombing in November 1987, and the British decision not to prosecute following the Stalker/Sampson inquiry into an alleged "shoot-to-kill" policy by the Royal Ulster Constabulary during 1982.

"*Officials may meet in subordinate groups*" This provision confirms that meetings of the Conference may take place without ministers though it suggests that such meetings are of lower standing than ministerial meetings. In practice meetings at official level are frequent and continuous contact and discussion is maintained through the Secretariat. For example, the proposals for legislation on fair employment had involved at least 15 meetings at official level by the end of 1988.

"*Membership of the conference and of sub-groups shall be small and flexible*" This provision appears to be intended to emphasise the practical character of the Conference at both ministerial and official level.

"*When the Conference meets at Ministerial level an Irish Minister designated as the Permanent Irish Ministerial Representative and the Secretary of State for Northern Ireland shall be joint Chairmen*" This provision would appear to rule out meetings at Ministerial level in the absence of the joint Chairmen, though there is an indication to the contrary in the following sentence. To date the designated Irish Minister has been the Minister for Foreign Affairs, initially Peter Barry and from March 1988, Brian Lenihan. It would be possible for the Irish Government to create a special ministerial post, such as "Minister for Northern Ireland", in order to emphasise its special role in respect of Northern Ireland under the Conference; a policy decision has been taken not to create such a ministerial post.

"*Within the framework of the Conference other Irish and British Ministers may hold or attend meetings as appropriate*" This provision makes it clear that other British and Irish ministers may attend "full" Conference meetings and also suggest that they may meet within the framework of the Conference but without the joint Chairmen. If the foregoing provision is to be strictly interpreted, such meetings would not constitute "meetings at Ministerial level". This view is borne out by the fact that the numbering of the meetings at Ministerial level in the published communiques does not include such meetings. Examples of the limited number of meetings between ministers of the two Governments which have taken place within the framework of the Conference but without the joint Chairmen include that between the Minister for Trade and Industry at the Northern Ireland Office and the Irish Ministers for Tourism and Transport and for Industry on July 29, 1987 and the meetings between the Minister for Agriculture at the Northern Ireland Office and the Irish Minister for Agriculture on October 12, 1987.

"*when legal matters are under consideration the Attorneys General may attend*" This additional provision may have been thought necessary given the special role of the law officers in the British and Irish constitutions. On the British side it is presumably the Attorney-General for Northern Ireland that is referred to, though in recent years the offices of Attorney-General for England and Wales and Attorney-General for Northern Ireland have been combined (Northern Ireland Constitution Act 1973, s.10). In practice, the Attorneys General have not attended meetings of the Conference since the 6th meeting on May 6, 1986; though the Irish Minister for Justice has been a regular participant on legal matters since then, there has been no parallel ministerial participant on the British side due to the absence of any minister for justice in Great Britain or Northern Ireland. Separate meetings between the Attorneys General have been held in respect of extradition, presumably within the framework of the Anglo-Irish Intergovernmental Council.

"*Ministers may be accompanied by their officials and their professional advisers*" The specific reference to professional advisers appears to have been intended primarily to permit the attendance of senior policemen and perhaps also soldiers, though none of the latter have yet attended a meeting.

"*for example, when questions of security policy or security co-operation are being discussed, they may be accompanied by the Commissioner of the Garda Síochána and the Chief Constable of the Royal Ulster Constabulary*" The Commissioner and the Chief Constable have been regular participants at meetings of the Conference, not least to emphasise that the widely reported rift between them before the establishment of the Conference had been healed. The practice has been for them to attend only that part of the meeting which deals with security matters.

"*or when questions of economic or social policy or co-operation are being discussed, they may be accompanied by officials of the relevant Departments*" This provision states the obvious and is a further example of the explanatory as opposed to formal or legalistic approach to the drafting of the Agreement.

"A Secretariat shall be established by the two Governments to service the Conference on a continuing basis in the discharge of its functions as set out in this Agreement" The creation of a permanent secretariat through which Irish officials might be more directly involved in the government of Northern Ireland was an important objective on the Irish side. The location of the Secretariat at Maryfield in Belfast was also an important symbol for nationalist supporters and for opponents of the Agreement. It should be noted, however, that there is no express provision either in the Agreement or in the communique of the summit meeting at which it was signed for any particular location. Since the choice of Maryfield was announced on the day the Agreement was signed, it seems likely that a provision for its location in Northern Ireland was removed from the draft Agreement at a late stage. There is therefore no formal obligation on either side to maintain the Secretariat at Maryfield. It might be moved to London or Dublin or become peripatetic without any breach or amendment of the Agreement. Though the operations of the Secretariat have been kept largely secret for security reasons, it has been revealed that the British side comprises three officials and six support staff (H. C. Deb. col. 831w (November 5, 1987)) and that the expenditure of United Kingdom funds on the Secretariat have been assessed at £468,000 (H. C. Deb. col. 80w (April 25, 1988)). Its primary function is to prepare papers and materials for meetings of the Conference. But it also serves as an important forum for discussion and channel of communication between the two Governments and as a useful source of information for the Irish Government on day-to-day events in Northern Ireland. In practice detailed views and proposals on many issues, including draft legislation, are submitted by the Irish side at this level. Its role may also be compared to that of the "incident centres" established in Belfast and elsewhere in Northern Ireland in 1976 in an effort to avoid the rapid escalation of communal tensions as a result of misunderstandings between the security forces, the government and members of the public.

Article 4

(a) In relation to matters coming within its field of activity, the Conference shall be a framework within which the United Kingdom Government and the Irish Government work together
  (i) for the accommodation of the rights and identities of the two traditions which exist in Northern Ireland; and
  (ii) for peace, stability and prosperity throughout the island of Ireland by promoting reconciliation, respect for human rights, co-operation against terrorism and the development of economic, social and cultural co-operation.
(b) It is the declared policy of the United Kingdom Government that responsibility in respect of certain matters within the powers of the Secretary of State for Northern Ireland should be devolved within Northern Ireland on a basis which would secure widespread acceptance throughout the community. The Irish Government support that policy.
(c) Both Governments recognise that devolution can be achieved only with the co-operation of constitutional representatives within Northern Ireland of both traditions there. The Conference shall be a framework within which the Irish Government may put forward views and proposals on the modalities of bringing about devolution in Northern Ireland, in so far as they relate to the interests of the minority community.

[This is the British version; in the Irish version precedence is given to the Irish Government.]

General Note

The first section of this Article sets out the main functions for the Conference, first, in respect of the internal Northern Ireland dimension and, secondly, in respect of the all-Ireland or north-south dimension in similar language to that used in the Preamble. The second and third sections make important statements in respect of the general objective of securing agreement on a form of devolved government for Northern Ireland. The achievement of this objective, as indicated elsewhere in the Agreement, would result in a substantial diminution in the functions of the Conference and might eventually lead to its disbandment as more and more of its functions were taken over by representatives of the two main communities in Northern Ireland, both in respect of its internal affairs and in respect of relations with the rest of

28

Ireland. Despite these provisions, however, the Conference has not yet spent much time on the pursuit of devolution as an objective.

ANNOTATIONS

"In relation to matters coming within its field of activity" As in other Articles, the drafters have been careful to limit the jurisdiction of the Conference to those matters expressly referred to in the Agreement.

"the Conference shall be a framework within which the United Kingdom Government and the Irish Government work together" This formulation emphasises that the Conference is intended as a procedure or a process for the joint pursuit of certain broad objectives rather than a body to implement clearly defined policies: see also Articles 5(c), 6 and 10(b).

"for the accommodation of the rights and identities of the two traditions which exist in Northern Ireland" This formulation follows closely the wording of the relevant paragraphs in the Preamble; the use of the word "traditions" instead of "communities" as in other references to Northern Ireland as opposed to Ireland as a whole is probably not of any significance; see the commentary on the Preamble. These matters are dealt with in greater detail in Article 5(a).

"for peace, stability and prosperity throughout the island of Ireland by promoting reconciliation, respect for human rights, co-operation against terrorism and the development of economic, social and cultural co-operation" This formulation of the general objectives of the Conference in relation to the whole island of Ireland, the north-south dimension, emphasises the potential for action in both parts of Ireland. There is no specific reference to the promotion of reconciliation in the Articles that follow. The protection of human rights is dealt with in Article 5(a), co-operation against terrorism in Article 9(a) and the development of economic, social and cultural co-operation in Article 10.

"It is the declared policy of the United Kingdom Government that responsibility in respect of certain matters within the powers of the Secretary of State for Northern Ireland should be devolved within Northern Ireland" This provision is merely a restatement of the current policy of the British Government and would not appear to impose any obligation on it not to change that policy. The most recent extended statement of governmental thinking was in the white paper *A Framework for Devolution* (Cmnd. 8541) published in 1982 in preparation for the re-establishment of the Northern Ireland Assembly under the Northern Ireland Act 1982. The broad framework for devolution under the terms of the Northern Ireland Constitution Act 1973 as amended by the Northern Ireland Act 1982 is explained in the annotation to Article 2 above.

"on a basis which would secure widespread acceptance throughout the community" This requirement has been consistently insisted upon by the British Government as a precondition to any form of executive or legislative devolution. Under the Northern Ireland Constitution Act 1973 the devolution of legislative and executive responsibility may be authorised only "if it appears to the Secretary of State . . . that a Northern Ireland Executive can be formed which, having regard to the support it commands in the Assembly and to the electorate on which that support is based, is likely to be widely accepted throughout the community, and that . . . there is a reasonable basis for the establishment in Northern Ireland of government by consent" (s.2(1)). Under the Northern Ireland Act 1982 an order for partial ("rolling") devolution may be made only if an order has been approved in both Houses of Parliament stating that its provisions are in the opinion of each House "likely to command widespread acceptance throughout the community" (s.2(2)); in addition, a proposal for such an order may be made only if *either* it has the support of at least 70 per cent. of the members of the Northern Ireland Assembly *or* it has the support of a simple majority and the Secretary of State is satisfied that in substance it is "likely to command widespread acceptance throughout the community" (s.1(4)); a similar test is imposed for the revocation of a partial devolution order (s.5(3)). It should be noted that under these provisions the test for the existence of "widespread acceptance throughout the community" is a discretionary assessment by the Secretary of State or Parliament. It is arguable that a weighted majority vote in a Northern Ireland Assembly or a referendum would be a clearer and more satisfactory test (see K. Boyle & T. Hadden, *Ireland: A Positive Proposal* (Penguin Books, 1985), pp. 83–84).

"The Irish Government support that policy" As in the case of the statement in respect of the policy of the British Government, this would not appear to impose any obligation on the Irish Government not to change its position; nor does it impose an obligation to take active steps to promote devolution. Though the provisions on devolution were apparently insisted on by the Irish side, in practice the Irish Government has not to date actively supported devolution of any kind.

"Both Governments recognise that devolution can be achieved only with the co-operation of constitutional representatives within Northern Ireland of both traditions there" This alternative formulation of the preconditions for devolution lays more emphasis on co-operation by parties representing both traditions in Northern Ireland. The use of the phrase "constitutional

representatives" may be taken to refer either to those elected by constitutional procedures or to those who accept the limitations imposed by constitutional procedures in the pursuit of their objectives. The phrase "constitutional parties" is popularly used to mean all parties which reject the use of violence. In the *New Ireland Forum Report* the phrase "democratic parties which reject violence" was used. It seems likely in the general context of the Agreement that the phrase was intended to mean the co-operation of the representatives of constitutional parties in this sense from both traditions, *i.e.* the major unionist parties, the Official Unionists and the Democratic Unionists, and the Social Democratic and Labour Party. The possibility that co-operation might be secured from one unionist party is not excluded. Whether the condition might be fulfilled by the co-operation of parties like the Alliance Party and the Workers Party which draw support from both communities is not clear. In any case the provision does not impose any binding obligation on either Government in that it merely states their recognition of what is asserted as a factual state of affairs.

"*The Conference shall be a framework within which the Irish Government may put forward views and proposals on the modalities of bringing about devolution in Northern Ireland in so far as they relate to the interests of the minority community*" This provision makes it clear that the Irish Government is regarded as having a legitimate interest in the form in which devolution might be introduced in Northern Ireland as guarantors of the interests of nationalists within Northern Ireland. This is in line with the broad structure of the Agreement, which gives the Irish Government a role as representatives of nationalists in Northern Ireland only until they can take over that role themselves within a fair system of regional government. The challenge in *McGimpsey & McGimpsey* v. *Ireland* (unreported, High Court, July 29, 1988) to the constitutionality of this role on the ground that it was discriminatory for the Irish Government to pursue the interests of only one section of the people of Northern Ireland was firmly rejected (see above). The use of the phrase "modalities of bringing about devolution" may be taken to refer both to the process by which devolution might be brought about and to the structure which should be adopted. In practice it does not appear that any views and proposals on this matter have actually been put forward by the Irish Government during the first three years of the Agreement.

C: POLITICAL MATTERS

Article 5

(a) The Conference shall concern itself with measures to recognise and accommodate the rights and identities of the two traditions in Northern Ireland, to protect human rights and to prevent discrimination. Matters to be considered in this area include measures to foster the cultural heritage of both traditions, changes in electoral arrangements, the use of flags and emblems, the avoidance of economic and social discrimination and the advantages and disadvantages of a Bill of Rights in some form in Northern Ireland.

(b) The discussion of these matters shall be mainly concerned with Northern Ireland, but the possible application of any measures pursuant to this Article by the Irish Government in their jurisdiction shall not be excluded.

(c) If it should prove impossible to achieve and sustain devolution on a basis which secures widespread acceptance in Northern Ireland, the Conference shall be a framework within which the Irish Government may, where the interests of the minority community are significantly or especially affected, put forward views on proposals for major legislation and on major policy issues, which are within the purview of the Northern Ireland Departments and which remain the responsibility of the Secretary of State for Northern Ireland.

ANNOTATIONS

"*The Conference shall concern itself with measures to recognise and accommodate the rights and identities of the two traditions in Northern Ireland*" The background to this general concern is discussed in the note to the relevant paragraph of the Preamble. There is a general and growing acceptance in many countries that the best approach to deep-seated ethnic, religious and cultural differences within a state is not to ignore them or attempt to suppress them but to permit those who wish to do so to express their separate identities within a broader context of democratic government within established jurisdictional boundaries. This has been expressed in general terms in Article 27 of the United Nations International Covenant on Civil and Political Rights:

> "In those states in which ethnic, religious or linguistic minorities exist, persons belonging to such minorities shall not be denied the right, in community with the other members of their group, to enjoy their own culture, to profess and practise their own religion, or to use their own language."

A more detailed account is given in the *Report of the Special Rapporteur to the United Nations Sub-Commission on Prevention of Discrimination and Protection of Minorities on the Rights of Persons Belonging to Ethnic, Religious and Linguistic Minorities* (Capotorti Report), United Nations 1979. Two broad approaches to this general problem may be identified. The first and more limited approach is to focus on the prohibition of any form of discrimination on ethnic, religious, linguistic or other grounds. But this negative or prohibitory approach, which was adopted in the Government of Ireland Act 1920 (s.5) and the Northern Ireland Constitution Act 1973 (ss.17 to 19) in respect of religious discrimination in Northern Ireland, may be combined with a policy of assimilation and does not necessarily ensure equal treatment or respect for the cultural or ethnic identity of minority groups. The second and more positive approach is to adopt measures designed to give full equality of treatment and esteem to members of all significant groups in political, social and economic terms. In many cases this may involve the provision of state funds on an equal or equitable basis for certain activities of importance to minority groups, notably in respect of education and linguistic and cultural expression. It is this second approach that appears to have been envisaged in respect of the two traditions or communities in Ireland by the *New Ireland Forum Report* and in Northern Ireland under the Anglo-Irish Agreement. But apart from the matters specifically referred to in the provisions that follow little or nothing has been done by the Conference to give substance to the recognition and accommodation of the rights and identities of both traditions within Northern Ireland, or for that matter in Ireland. No views or proposals have been put forward on general constitutional provisions which might help to ensure equality of treatment of the two traditions, on ways in which those in Northern Ireland who assert Irish nationality might be facilitated in doing so, on ways in which the use of the Irish language on official papers or in other ways might be facilitated, or on the promotion of Irish and Gaelic culture through officially supported or recognised media such as radio and television. Matters of this kind have been expressly provided for in other jurisdictions in which there are ethnically, linguistically or culturally diverse groups, such as Wales, Canada and Belgium, and figured prominently in the draft convention for the protection of minorities published by the Minority Rights Group (*The International Protection of Minorities*, Report No. 41 (1979)).

"*to protect human rights*" This provision is not specifically linked to Northern Ireland and might therefore have application in Ireland as well as Northern Ireland. At the 9th meeting of the Conference on October 6, 1986 the British Government indicated that while they saw some difficulties with the Irish proposal for a Bill of Rights for Northern Ireland they were prepared to consider some form of joint declaration of rights by both Governments. This idea has not been pursued. For a general discussion of the protection of human rights in both parts of Ireland, and in Britain, see S. Bailey (ed.), *Human Rights and Responsibilities in Britain and Ireland: A Christian Perspective* (1988).

"*and to prevent discrimination*" As with the preceding provision this is not specifically linked to Northern Ireland and might therefore have application in Ireland as a whole. The measures discussed in respect of Northern Ireland are noted below.

"*Matters to be considered in this area include*" Three of the items which follow were already on the intergovernmental agenda when the Agreement was drafted (as noted in the comment on each below). As indicated above, no other items of substance have since been added.

"*measures to foster the cultural heritage of both traditions*" The issue which had been given most prominence in this respect before the Agreement was the prohibition on the use of street names in Irish under the Public Health and Local Government (Miscellaneous Provisions) Act (Northern Ireland) 1949, s.19(4). The general issue of the use of the Irish language in Northern Ireland was discussed at the 7th meeting of the Conference on June 17, 1986 at which the British side suggested the possible use of dual language in specific areas where the local community so desired, the need for more accurate information on the actual use of Irish in Northern Ireland and possible financial support for cultural activities in the Irish language. No action has yet been taken on the use of Irish in street names, but a report on the use of Irish in Northern Ireland has been completed by the officially funded Policy, Planning and Research Unit: *The Irish Language in Northern Ireland 1987: Preliminary Report of a Survey of Knowledge, Interest and Ability* (Occasional Paper No. 17, 1988).

"changes in electoral arrangements" This item refers to the fact that certain Irish citizens not born in Northern Ireland or resident there for seven years were excluded from voting in elections for local government and the Northern Ireland Parliament and Assembly under the provisions of the Electoral Law Act (Northern Ireland) 1962, though they were entitled to vote in elections for the Westminster Parliament both in Britain and in Northern Ireland; such persons are referred to in the electoral lists in Northern Ireland as "I" voters, though the use of the letter "I" refers not to their Irish citizenship but to the limitation of their franchise to elections for the Imperial Parliament. This anomaly was raised in the Anglo-Irish Joint Studies in 1981, when it was estimated that some 5,000–6,000 people might be affected. The issue was discussed at the 6th and 7th meetings of the Conference on May 9, 1986 and June 17, 1986. Following this, action was taken to extend the franchise for elections to the Northern Ireland Assembly under the Northern Ireland Assembly Elections (Amendment) Order 1986 (S.I. No. 1811 of 1986). Action to remove the anomaly in respect of local government elections was not taken until 1988. At the 23rd meeting of the Conference on July 27, 1988 the British Government restated its intention to enact appropriate legislation. This was finally introduced in the Elected Authorities (Northern Ireland) Bill 1988, which also makes provision for candidates for election to local authorities to make a declaration that they do not support violence. It has been estimated that some 10,000 "I" voters will be enfranchised under this legislation for the local government elections due in May 1989. The lengthy delay in implementing these measures on the British side may be contrasted with the action taken in 1985 in Ireland to grant equivalent voting rights to British citizens in Ireland to those enjoyed by Irish citizens in Britain, currently under the Representation of the People Act 1983.

"the use of flags and emblems" This refers to the provisions of the Flags and Emblems (Display) Act (Northern Ireland) 1954 which was enacted to discourage the display of the Irish flag in Northern Ireland, though in formal legal terms it merely gave special protection to the display of the British flag despite any risk of public disorder which might result. The statute was repealed under the Public Order (Northern Ireland) Order 1986. The issue was raised and discussed at the 5th meeting of the Conference on March 11, 1986 and the 11th meeting on December 8, 1986.

"the avoidance of economic and social discrimination" The prevention of discrimination in employment in Northern Ireland on religious grounds has been regularly discussed at recent meetings of the Conference. It was first raised at the 9th meeting on July 29, 1986 following the publication of the discussion paper on *Equality of Opportunity* by the Department of Economic Development for Northern Ireland which confirmed that despite the work of the Fair Employment Agency under the Fair Employment (Northern Ireland) Act 1976 there remained substantial differences in employment and unemployment rates for Catholics and Protestants. It was subsequently discussed at the 13th meeting on April 22, 1987, the 15th meeting on October 21, 1987, the 19th meeting on February 24, 1988, the 21st meeting on May 5, 1988, the 22nd meeting on June 17, 1988 and the 23rd meeting on July 27, 1988. The major pressures for action on this issue, however, have been made by the supporters of the McBride Principles in the United States and by the *Report on Fair Employment* by the Standing Advisory Commission on Human Rights (Cm. 237, 1987), leading to the publication in May 1988 by the Secretary of State for Northern Ireland of a white paper *Fair Employment in Northern Ireland* (Cm. 380) with a view to legislation in 1989. The discussions at the Conference have been largely in response to these separate developments. There has been no discussion of other forms of discrimination, either in Northern Ireland or in the rest of Ireland.

"and the advantages and disadvantages of a Bill of Rights in some form in Northern Ireland" This issue was raised at the 9th meeting of the Conference on October 6, 1986 at which the British side indicated that there would be difficulties in adopting the Irish proposals but that some form of joint declaration on the effective protection of human rights might be considered. The idea was not pursued, probably because any such joint declaration would be legally irrelevant. The difficulties on the British side would appear to relate to the continuing debate in Britain over the desirability of incorporating into British law the European Convention on Human Rights and Fundamental Freedoms, of which both the United Kingdom and Ireland are signatories. The British view appears to be that it would be wrong to incorporate the Convention into Northern Ireland law unless and until the same was done in the United Kingdom as a whole, not least because to do so might result in some Westminster legislation being declared unlawful by the courts in Northern Ireland while it remained valid in the rest of the United Kingdom. The arguments in favour of a separate Bill of Rights for Northern Ireland were extensively reviewed by the Standing Advisory Commission for Human Rights in 1977 in *The Protection of Human Rights by Law in Northern Ireland* (Cmnd. 7009): the Commission concluded that "there are important legal and constitutional considerations which would make an exclusively Northern Ireland Bill both inappropriate and undesirable in the context of the existing constitutional framework of the United Kingdom" (paras. 3.0 and

4.07). This is an odd conclusion given that a number of special protections of the kind that would be included in any Bill of Rights were inserted into both the Government of Ireland Act 1920 and the Northern Ireland Constitution Act 1973, Part III. Though there would be some constitutional difficulties in entrenching any such Bill against future repeal by the Westminster Parliament, these are not insuperable. An interpretative provision to safeguard the Canadian Bill of Rights against implied as opposed to express repeal was adopted in Canada in 1960 and a similar strategy was proposed for the United Kingdom in a bill promoted by Lord Broxbourne and others in 1986. Clause 4(2) of the Human Rights and Fundamental Freedoms Bill provided that:

"Any enactment made or passed after the passing of this Act which authorises or requires any act to be done shall be taken to authorise or require that act to be done only in a manner and to the extent that it does not infringe any of the fundamental rights and freedoms of any person within the jurisdiction of the United Kingdom, save in so far as such enactment is an Act which expressly directs that this subsection shall not apply to the doing of the act in question or is made pursuant to a power conferred by an Act which expressly so directs."

Any such Bill of Rights might also be given some protection against future repeal by means of an international treaty between the United Kingdom and Ireland or other interested states.

"The discussion of these matters shall be mainly concerned with Northern Ireland, but the possible application of any measures pursuant to this Article by the Irish Government in their jurisdiction shall not be excluded" This provision is in line with the general structure of the Agreement, as set out in Article 2(b), in giving precedence to the internal Northern Ireland dimension but at the same time suggesting possible co-operative action on a North/South basis. On a strict interpretation of the wording in this section, notably the omission of the word "co-operative," independent action in Ireland to protect human rights and to prevent discrimination might also be discussed. A positive approach to the protection of human rights and to the prevention of discrimination in Ireland might be thought to require some action to take account of the interests of minorities, including the Protestant minority. In formal terms, human rights in the Republic in certain respects are less well-protected than in Northern Ireland. Ireland has a written constitution with a "Bill of Rights" but the Constitution also precludes any possibility of divorce and its recognition of the right to life of the unborn renders abortion unlawful in all circumstances. There is an official censorship board with powers to ban books deemed obscene or which advocate abortion. The Constitution does outlaw religious discrimination but only discriminatory action by governmental authority; religiously motivated discrimination by private persons is not unlawful. There is no anti-discrimination legislation whether on grounds of race, religion or belief. Ireland has yet to ratify the United Nations Covenants of 1966, the Covenant on Civil and Political Rights and the Covenant on Economic, Social and Cultural Rights although ratification is expected in 1989. The Convention on the Elimination of Racial Discrimination has been signed but not ratified. These instruments of international human rights law have been ratified by the British Government and their protections extend to Northern Ireland.

"If it should prove impossible to achieve and sustain devolution on a basis which secures widespread acceptance in Northern Ireland" This provision makes it clear that if agreement on devolution in Northern Ireland cannot be reached, as provided for in Article 4, or if an agreed structure for devolution breaks down, as in the case of the power-sharing executive in 1974, the Conference shall continue or resume its role in respect of the internal Northern Ireland dimension.

"the Conference shall be a framework" For a discussion of this phrase see the comment on Article 4(a).

"within which the Irish Government may, where the interests of the minority community are significantly or especially affected, put forward views on proposals for major legislation and on major policy issues" This formulation of the role of the Irish Government is more restrictive than in some other Articles, in that it expressly limits the right of the Irish side to put forward views on major legislation and major policy issues where the interests of the minority are significantly affected. In so doing it emphasises that the Irish Government's role in the Conference is to represent the interests of the minority community rather than to discuss with the British side all aspects of the government of Northern Ireland. As noted above, the challenge to the constitutionality of this role on the ground that it is discriminatory for the Irish Government to pursue the interests of only one section of the community in Northern Ireland was firmly rejected by Barrington J. in *McGimpsey & McGimpsey* v. *Ireland* (unreported, High Court, July 29, 1988). An important example is the issue of high unemployment in minority areas, particularly West Belfast. Repeated representations on this matter by the Irish side have clearly influenced the British Government's decision to introduce a package of measures to promote economic activity in West Belfast: see the communiques of March 25, 1988, May 5, 1988, June 17, 1988, July 22, 1988, and December 14, 1988.

"*which are within the purview of the Northern Ireland Departments and which remain the responsibility of the Secretary of State for Northern Ireland*" This provision emphasises that the jurisdiction of the Conference is limited to matters dealt with on a purely Northern Ireland basis, thus excluding matters dealt with on a United Kingdom basis such as defence, foreign affairs, taxation and an increasing range of financial and commercial matters. Such matters in so far as they concern the Irish Government might be dealt with within the framework of the Anglo-Irish Intergovernmental Council.

Article 6

The Conference shall be a framework within which the Irish Government may put forward views and proposals on the role and composition of bodies appointed by the Secretary of State for Northern Ireland or by Departments subject to his direction and control including
the Standing Advisory Commission on Human Rights;
the Fair Employment Agency;
the Equal Opportunities Commission;
the Police Authority for Northern Ireland;
the Police Complaints Board.

ANNOTATIONS

"*The Conference shall be a framework within which the Irish Government may put forward views and proposals*" For a discussion of this formulation see the comments on Articles 2(b) and 4(a) above.

"*on the role and composition of bodies appointed by the Secretary of State for Northern Ireland or by Departments subject to his direction and control*" The use of the word "role" in addition to "composition" is presumably intended to give a wider frame of reference to the provision. Although the role of most of the bodies concerned is defined by statute it may be argued that the right of the Irish Government under this Article is wider than that under Article 5(c) which is limited to views and proposals on major legislation or policy issues of special concern to the minority community. The main purpose of this provision is to enable the Irish Government to put forward names for appointment to official bodies subject to the Northern Ireland Office or Northern Ireland Departments. It may be presumed, though it is not expressly stated, that this is designed to ensure that the bodies shall have a reasonable proportion of members from or acceptable to the minority community. It has been stated in answer to a Parliamentary Question that in the period up to March 9, 1988 the names of 39 persons had been put forward by the Irish Government, of whom 19 already held positions on relevant bodies. At that date 12 people suggested by the Irish held a total of 20 public appointments (H.C. Deb. col. 230w (March 9, 1988)). The Northern Ireland Office has for a number of years maintained a register of persons willing to accept appointment to official bodies and has sought nominations from a wide range of voluntary bodies. It is clear that in respect of appointments made directly by the Secretary of State the role of the Irish Government is to continue indefinitely. The use of the phrase "Departments subject to his direction and control" is presumably intended to exclude Northern Ireland Departments in respect of which responsibility has been devolved in accordance with Article 4.

"*including the Standing Advisory Commission on Human Rights*" This body was established under section 20 of the Northern Ireland Constitution Act 1973 for the purpose of "advising the Secretary of State on the adequacy and effectiveness of the law for the time being in force in preventing discrimination on the grounds of religious belief or political opinion and in providing redress for persons aggrieved by discrimination on either ground." It has with the consent of the Secretary of State adopted a somewhat more general advisory role in respect of human rights of all kinds. But it has no executive functions of any kind and does not pursue individual cases. The Northern Ireland Commissioner for Complaints, the Northern Ireland Parliamentary Commissioner for Administration and the Chairman of the Fair Employment Agency are *ex officio* members and the remaining members and the chairman are appointed by the Secretary of State.

"*the Fair Employment Agency*" The Agency was established under the Fair Employment (Northern Ireland) Act 1976 to receive and investigate individual complaints of discrimination in employment and to carry out general investigations into the extent of equality of opportunity in employment. Its members are appointed by the Head of the Department of Economic Development; out of a maximum total of a chairman and 11 members, three each are nominated by the Northern Ireland Committee of the Irish Congress of Trade Unions and by employers' organisations in Northern Ireland. The Agency is to be replaced by a Fair

Employment Commission with somewhat wider powers under new legislation promised in the white paper *Fair Employment in Northern Ireland* (Cm. 380).

"*the Equal Opportunities Commission*" The Equal Opportunities Commission for Northern Ireland was established under the Sex Discrimination (Northern Ireland) Order 1976, s.54 and has a similar role in relation to discrimination on grounds of sex. Its members were initially appointed by the head of the Department of Manpower Services, and currently by the Department of Economic Development (see Departments (Northern Ireland) Order 1982, art. 3).

"*the Police Authority for Northern Ireland*" The Police Authority was established under the Police Act (Northern Ireland) 1970 as an independent body to maintain an adequate and efficient police force. It has the power to appoint and dismiss the Chief Constable and other senior officers and to hold inquiries into matters of public concern. Its members are appointed by the Secretary of State who is required to secure in so far as is possible that the membership is representative of the community in Northern Ireland and also of a number of specified bodies and interests such as local authorities and other public bodies, the legal profession, trade unions, agriculture, industry and commerce and youth organisations.

"*the Police Complaints Board*" The Board was established under the Police (Northern Ireland) Order 1977 to review the handling by the Chief Constable of complaints against the police. It has been replaced by a somewhat more independent supervisory body, the Independent Commission for Police Complaints for Northern Ireland, under the Police (Northern Ireland) Order 1987. The members of both bodies were or are appointed by the Secretary of State.

D: SECURITY AND RELATED MATTERS

Article 7

(*a*) The Conference shall consider
   (i) security policy;
   (ii) relations between the security forces and the community;
   (iii) prisons policy.
(*b*) The Conference shall consider the security situation at its regular meetings and thus provide an opportunity to address policy issues, serious incidents and forthcoming events.
(*c*) The two Governments agree that there is a need for a programme of special measures in Northern Ireland to improve relations between the security forces and the community, with the object in particular of making the security forces more readily accepted by the nationalist community. Such a programme shall be developed for the Conference's consideration, and may include the establishment of local consultative machinery, training in community relations, crime prevention schemes involving the community, improvements in arrangements for handling complaints, and action to increase the proportion of members of the minority in the Royal Ulster Constabulary. Elements of the programme may be considered by the Irish Government suitable for application within their jurisdiction.
(*d*) The Conference may consider policy issues relating to prisons. Individual cases may be raised as appropriate, so that information can be provided or inquiries instituted.

GENERAL NOTE

The concerns of the two Governments on security matters are at one level identical in that both are committed, as set out in the Preamble, to working together to ensure that those who attempt to pursue political objectives by violent means do not succeed. But there has always been considerable difference in emphasis as to how this objective is to be achieved. The British Government has generally been concerned to secure what it considers to be maximum effectiveness in the prevention of terrorism and the conviction of terrorists both within Northern Ireland and in respect of cross-border terrorist activity. The Irish Government has generally laid more emphasis on the general acceptability of security measures to members of the minority community in Northern Ireland, on the ground that general acceptance within Northern Ireland of both political and legal structures and of security operations is an essential precondition of the elimination of terrorist activity and other forms of politically motivated violence. The provisions of Article 7, particularly those of paragraph (c), are predominantly related to this latter concern. Those of Article 9 in respect of cross-border co-operation on security are more directly related to the former.

ANNOTATIONS

"The Conference shall consider" This formulation makes it clear that the consideration of security is mandatory and not like many other aspects of the work of the Conference dependent on the putting forward of views and proposals by the Irish Government. In practice security has been considered at almost every meeting of the Conference, though the prominence of that part of the agenda has varied. The Chief Constable of the Royal Ulster Constabulary and the Commissioner of the Garda Síochána have been present at 14 out of the first 25 meetings of the Conference.

"(i) security policy" The application of this is spelled out in paragraph (b) below.

"(ii) relations between the security forces and the community" The application of this is spelled out in paragraph (c) below.

"(iii) prisons policy" The application of this is spelled out in paragraph (d) below.

"The Conference shall consider the security situation at its regular meetings" As noted above this imposes an obligation on the Conference to consider security at all but special meetings called under the terms of Article 3. In practice the majority of special meetings have also been primarily concerned with security. Though specific provision is made in respect of cross-border security under Article 9, the obligation under this paragraph is not limited to the situation within Northern Ireland.

"and thus provide an opportunity to address policy issues" In this and in other provisions, notably Articles 7(d) and 9(b), a distinction is drawn between issues of policy and operational decisions. The intention is to emphasise the general principle that responsibility for decision-making in each jurisdiction is exclusively a matter for the respective Governments as set out in Article 2.

"serious incidents" This may be taken to refer both to the consideration of serious incidents at ministerial meetings whether regular or specially convened, as in the case of the special meeting summoned on November 16, 1987 after the Enniskillen bombing, and also the consideration by the Conference Secretariat of such incidents on a more regular basis. The objective of the latter is to ensure that representatives of both Governments have access to information and official thinking in the immediate aftermath of major incidents and to avoid damaging confrontations in statements to the media on either side. This latter function may be compared with that of the "incident centres" set up after the ending of internment in 1975 with a view to ensuring more effective and immediate communication between the security forces and local community representatives in nationalist areas and thus to avoiding the escalation of tension and confrontation based on mutual misunderstandings.

"and forthcoming events" This may be taken to refer specifically to the discussion of policy in respect of marches, funerals and other gatherings which may be expected to create a risk of confrontation between the security forces and local communities. The Conference was clearly involved in the discussion of policy in respect of Orange Order marches in Portadown in the summer of 1986, though no reference was made to this specific matter in any of the formal communiques of ministerial meetings, perhaps in order to avoid any implication of interference in operational decisions contrary to the terms of Article 9(2). The tension between the desire of the Irish Government to show that it has had some influence on decisions on such matters and the desire of the British Government and of the Chief Constable to maintain the principle of exclusive responsibility has been a major difficulty in this context.

"The two Governments agree that there is a need for a programme of special measures in Northern Ireland to improve relations between the security forces and the community" Though this provision is drafted as a statement of fact, the following sentence makes clear that it imposes an obligation on both sides. Unlike the other provisions in this Article the programme is specifically tied to measures within Northern Ireland, with a proviso, similar to that in Article 2, that some elements may apply in Ireland. The use of the phrase "special measures" indicates that the programme is likely to include more than the ordinary provisions designed to improve relations between the police and the community in Britain and the rest of Ireland.

"with the object in particular of making the security forces more readily accepted by the nationalist community" The increasing alienation of the nationalist community in Northern Ireland from both the British Army and the Royal Ulster Constabulary was a major theme of the *New Ireland Forum Report* (see Chap. 3). Though the arrival of British troops in Northern Ireland in 1969 was generally welcomed by nationalists the relationship between them soon deteriorated due to a succession of policies and incidents, notably the introduction of internment in

1971, the policy of mass "screening" in nationalist areas from the early 1970s, the Bloody Sunday shootings in Derry on January 30, 1972, when 13 civilians were shot dead by paratroops, the use of the "five techniques" of interrogation in depth in 1971 and of apparently systematic ill-treatment during interrogation in the period from 1976–78, the succession of "shoot-to-kill" incidents in 1978 and 1982, and the failure of the authorities to prosecute or secure convictions against those responsible for more than a handful of the proven or alleged abuses. A major underlying problem is the absence of any significant participation by members of the minority community in the police or the locally recruited Ulster Defence Regiment of the British Army, with the result that all policing and security operations are seen as being imposed by alien forces.

"such a programme shall be developed for the Conference's consideration" This provision makes it clear, as noted above, that there is a joint obligation to prepare a programme of special measures, subject to the final proviso that this does not oblige the British Government to accept it. In practice no such general programme appears to have been prepared, though the matter was regularly raised in the first year of the Conference, at the 1st, 5th, 7th, 9th and 11th meetings. The main focus of attention in this initial period was the commitment by the British Government in the communique of the Hillsborough summit to ensure that Ulster Defence Regiment and Army patrols were accompanied by uniformed RUC officers. Since then the matter has been less frequently discussed and the particular measures covered, the introduction of a code of conduct for the RUC at the 15th meeting on October 21, 1987 and the new police complaints procedure at the 23rd meeting on July 27, 1988, were merely the extension to the RUC of measures already in operation in Britain.

"and may include the establishment of local consultative machinery" The only formal measure to this end which has emerged is the extension to Northern Ireland under the proposed Police and Criminal Evidence (Northern Ireland) Order of the provisions under the equivalent British legislation for the Police Authority to make arrangements to obtain the views of people about policing and their co-operation in preventing crime (art. 82); for the equivalent British provisions see the Police and Criminal Evidence Act 1984, s.106. No special measures have apparently been discussed to meet the particular problems of police liaison with the community in Northern Ireland.

"training in community relations" No special measures have been specified in Conference communiques or otherwise publicised under this heading, other than general references to the importance of community relations in the RUC Code of Conduct.

"crime prevention schemes involving the community" No special measures have been specified in Conference communiques or otherwise publicised under this heading, though provision is made for consultation on such schemes under the proposed Police and Criminal Evidence (Northern Ireland) Order (art. 82) (see above).

"improvements in arrangements for handling complaints" As noted above under Article 6, new provisions to ensure more independent supervision of the handling of police complaints were introduced under the Police (Northern Ireland) Order 1987. This was discussed at the 11th meeting of the Conference on December 8, 1986. The only major difference between the provisions of the Order and the equivalent British provisions under Part IX of the Police and Criminal Evidence Act 1984 is the right of the Secretary of State or the Police Authority to refer to the Commission any matter which appears to indicate that a member of the police force may have committed a criminal offence or an offence against discipline and is not the subject of a complaint (see Police (Northern Ireland) Order 1987, art. 8(2)).

"and action to increase the proportion of members of the minority in the Royal Ulster Constabulary" Though detailed statistics are not published it is generally accepted that fewer than 10 per cent. of some 11,250 full-time and 1,650 part-time officers in the RUC (1987 figures) are members of the minority community. The continuing low level of recruitment among Catholics is due in part to the continuing campaign by the IRA against Catholic RUC officers, in part to the resulting need for Catholic members of the RUC to cut themselves off from their communities and in part to a feeling among many Catholics that the RUC remains an essentially Protestant force. No special measures to deal with these problems have been specified in Conference communiques or otherwise publicised.

"Elements of the programme may be considered by the Irish Government suitable for application within their jurisdiction" This provision reflects the similar general provision for reciprocal action under Article 2. It is not made clear precisely what measures by the Irish Government might help to improve relationships between the security forces and the nationalist community in Northern Ireland, though many of the elements in such a programme might well be desirable in their own right. No detailed proposals in this context have emerged in Conference communiques. One possible way of increasing confidence in the RUC among nationalists would be to increase general contacts between the two forces, by way of shared training facilities, exchanges of personnel and reciprocal action on such matters as the

appointment of a senior officer from another force to carry out an inquiry into alleged mal-practice. The presence of a few officers from the Garda Síochána in police stations in Northern Ireland and of officers from the RUC in the rest of Ireland, provided that it was arranged on a clearly reciprocal basis, might assist in breaking down psychological barriers on both sides and in so doing help to increase the prospects for greater recruitment of nationalists in Northern Ireland to the RUC.

"The Conference may consider policy issues relating to prisons" This provision makes a similar distinction to that in paragraph (b) between the discussion of policy and of operational decisions; see also Articles 2 and 9(b). But the line is a fine one. In practice what little discussion there has been of prisons in Conference meetings has been directed at obtaining information, as provided below, rather than matters of general policy: at the 2nd (special) meeting of the Conference on December 30, 1985 the facts relating to the then current hunger strike at the Maze Prison were conveyed to the Irish side; at the 20th meeting on March 25, 1988 and the 23rd meeting on July 27, 1988 brief reference was made to a review of the position of young offenders held at the Secretary of State's pleasure.

"Individual cases may be raised as appropriate, so that information can be provided or inquiries instituted" This provision fulfils the same function in respect of prisoners as that for the exchange of information on serious incidents under paragraph (b). The wording indicates that it would not be appropriate for specific recommendations in relation to individual prisoners to be put forward by the Irish side in respect of persons in prison in Northern Ireland or by the British side in respect of persons in prison in the rest of Ireland. Though the paragraph is not restricted to Northern Ireland, or to Ireland as a whole, the general structure of the Agreement would appear to exclude the use of the Conference, as opposed to the Anglo-Irish Intergovernmental Council, for the provision of information or the institution of inquiries about Irish prisoners in Britain.

E: LEGAL MATTERS, INCLUDING THE ADMINISTRATION OF JUSTICE

Article 8

The Conference shall deal with issues of concern to both countries relating to the enforcement of the criminal law. In particular it shall consider whether there are areas of the criminal law applying in the North and in the South respectively which might with benefit be harmonised. The two Governments agree on the importance of public confidence in the administration of justice. The Conference shall seek, with the help of advice from experts as appropriate, measures which would give substantial expression to this aim, considering *inter alia* the possibility of mixed courts in both jurisdictions for the trial of certain offences. The Conference shall also be concerned with policy aspects of extradition and extra-territorial jurisdiction as between North and South.

GENERAL NOTE

There has long been a marked difference in emphasis by the two Governments on how to combat terrorism in Northern Ireland. The British Government has generally taken the view that very substantial changes in the ordinary common law and statutory rules for the trial of offenders in Northern Ireland have been made necessary by the extent of paramilitary activity, not least the widespread intimidation of potential witnesses and of jurors and the sustained attacks, both physical and in propaganda, against the whole legal system by the Provisional IRA and its supporters. This approach was most clearly enunciated in the *Report of the Diplock Committee on Legal Procedures to Deal with Terrorist Activities in Northern Ireland* (Cmnd. 5815, 1972), which led to the introduction of a wide range of emergency provisions under the Northern Ireland (Emergency Provisions) Act 1973. These included not only the continued provision for detention without trial, though that has not been used since 1975, but also provision for the trial of "scheduled" offences before a single judge without a jury in so-called "Diplock Courts," and for the removal of some common law restraints on the admissibility of evidence obtained under the prolonged interrogation of suspects which was also provided for both in the Northern Ireland (Emergency Provisions) Acts and, from 1974, in the Prevention of Terrorism (Temporary Provisions) Acts. Despite a number of critical official and international inquiries into alleged abuses of these provisions the system introduced in 1972 has remained essentially intact (see now Northern Ireland (Emergency Provisions) Acts 1978 and 1987 and the Prevention of Terrorism (Temporary Provisions) Act 1984). Though broadly similar provisions have for many years been available in Ireland under the Offences Against the State Act 1939, the Irish Government has repeatedly expressed its concern over the operation of the judicial system in Northern Ireland, notably over the almost exclusive reliance in Diplock trials on confessions, some of which have been obtained in disputed circumstances, the systematic reliance on "supergrass" evidence without corroboration in the period from 1980 to 1985 and the general failure of the authorities to prosecute and the courts to convict soldiers and policemen allegedly involved in unlawful interrogation practices or in alleged "shoot-to-kill" policies.

The continuing differences of approach in respect of the extradition of suspected terrorists from Ireland to Great Britain and Northern Ireland which first came to prominence during the Sunningdale Conference and the ensuing *Report of the Law Enforcement Commission* (Cmnd. 5627; Prl. 3832) (see Introduction) are in part related to these general concerns among nationalists in Ireland about the quality of justice in trials of terrorist suspects in British and Northern Ireland courts and in part to more general problems over the "political offence" rule, as discussed in detail in Chapter 4 below.

This Article sets out to resolve these differences of approach by giving general jurisdiction to the Conference over all aspects of the enforcement of the criminal law, including extradition and extra-territorial jurisdiction, and by focusing attention on the need to secure public confidence in the administration of justice. It also suggests two possible measures by which this objective might be pursued: first, by the harmonisation of the criminal law in both parts of Ireland and, secondly, by the creation of mixed courts, *i.e.* courts composed of judges from both jurisdictions, to deal with certain offences.

ANNOTATIONS

"The Conference shall deal with issues of concern to both countries relating to the enforcement of the criminal law" This provision is drafted in the broadest terms and imposes an obligation on both sides to discuss the issues. It is not explicitly restricted to Northern Ireland or Ireland as a whole, though in the general context of the Agreement it must be taken not to include issues of concern within Britain. The use of the words "both countries" suggests a wider coverage than the words "both Governments" which are used elsewhere in the Agreement, though the difference may not have been intended. "The enforcement of the criminal law" clearly covers not only both terrorist and ordinary crimes, but also both procedural and substantive issues. But all matters of civil law, both substantive and procedural, are clearly excluded. The general harmonisation of the law in Northern Ireland with that in the rest of Ireland is not within the jurisdiction of the Conference, though it was suggested as a feasible objective in a study for the New Ireland Forum: see K. Boyle and D. Greer, *The Legal System, North and South* (1984).

"In particular it shall consider whether there are areas of the criminal law applying in the North and in the South respectively which might with benefit be harmonised" The purpose of harmonising the criminal law, both in substance and in procedure, in the context of this Article might be partly to avoid disputes over the merits of particular provisions on either side and partly to facilitate the introduction of mixed courts, as suggested in the *Report of the Law Enforcement Commission* in 1974 (Cmnd. 5627; Prl. 3832, para. 39). The possibility of harmonising the operation of special courts for terrorist offences by providing for three judges to sit in Diplock trials as in the Special Criminal Court in Dublin has frequently been raised but has never appeared in any formal communique. More general references were made in the communiques of the 4th and 5th meetings of the Conference on February 13, 1986 and March 11, 1986 to a report by officials on other aspects of possible harmonisation. But nothing further has emerged on this matter. The use of the words "the North" and "the South" for Northern Ireland and the rest of Ireland appears only in this Article and Article 10(c); like others writing about the two parts of Ireland the drafters appear to have abandoned the attempt to avoid these colloquial though constitutionally doubtful expressions.

"The two Governments agree on the importance of public confidence in the administration of justice" This provision, like a number of others in the Agreement, is a statement of the current position of the two Governments and does not in itself have any binding or obligatory force.

"The Conference shall seek, with the help of advice from experts as appropriate, measures which would give substantial expression to this aim" This provision imposes an obligation on the Conference to seek practical means of securing public confidence in the administration of justice. The reference to the possible use of experts may have been incorporated with the *Report of the Law Enforcement Commission* set up at the Sunningdale Conference in 1973 (see above) in mind. No such advice or assistance has in practice been sought from experts outside the body of officials involved in the work of the Conference. The importance to the

39

Irish Government of securing agreement on some substantial measures to increase the confidence of nationalists in the judicial system in Northern Ireland was emphasised by the inclusion of an explicit reference to it in the formal communique of the summit meeting at Hillsborough on November 15, 1985 and by subsequent references by the then Taoiseach, Dr Fitzgerald, to an understanding that the accession by the Irish Government to the European Convention on the Suppression of Terrorism (see below) was linked to progress in this field, notably in respect of the introduction of three-judge courts and the ending of reliance on the uncorroborated evidence of supergrasses in Diplock trials. Though no action has yet been taken on the first of these objectives, the second has in practice been achieved partly by a series of decisions in the Northern Ireland Court of Appeal setting aside convictions on the uncorroborated evidence of accomplices and partly by a tacit decision by the British Attorney-General not to pursue new cases on such evidence: see the communique of the 11th meeting of the Conference on December 8, 1986 and S. Greer, "Supergrasses and the Legal System in Britain and Northern Ireland" (1986) *Law Quarterly Review* 198; for a detailed account of the practicalities of introducing three-judge courts see the report by J. Jackson for the Standing Advisory Commission on Human Rights, *Annual Report for 1985–86*, Appendix D.

"*considering inter alia the possibility of mixed courts in both jurisdictions for the trial of certain offences*" The concept of a mixed court may be taken to refer to a court with a panel of judges drawn from both Northern Ireland and Ireland: see the general discussion in the *Report of the Law Enforcement Commission* (Cmnd. 5627; Prl. 3832, Chap. 5). The idea was revived by Dr Fitzgerald in the November 1982 Irish General Election campaign. It might be most appropriate and most readily acceptable in respect of offences committed in a cross-border security zone in which joint patrols by the RUC and the Garda Síochána were permitted and perhaps also offences in respect of which the provisions for extradition or extra-territorial jurisdiction might apply (see below and Chapter 4). The possibility of such mixed courts does not appear to have been actively pursued in the Conference.

"*The Conference shall also be concerned with policy aspects of extradition and extra-territorial jurisdiction as between North and South*" As in other Articles, a clear distinction is drawn between policy on these matters and decisions on individual cases which are not within the jurisdiction of the Conference, either because they are judicial decisions or because they fall under the general provisions of Article 2 reserving exclusive responsibility for governmental decisions within each jurisdiction. Policy aspects of extradition and extra-territorial jurisdiction between Ireland and Great Britain are not included, and should strictly be dealt with in the framework of the Anglo-Irish Intergovernmental Council. In practice these matters have been discussed both within the Conference with the respective Attorneys-General present (see the communiques of the 4th meeting on February 13, 1986 and the 6th meeting on May 9, 1986) and more recently at official and ministerial level within the Conference (see the communiques of the 20th meeting on March 25, 1988 and the 22nd meeting on June 17, 1988) in the light of separate meetings between the Attorneys-General presumably within the framework of the Anglo-Irish Intergovernmental Council on May 11, 1988 and July 18, 1988. The interrelationship between extradition, *i.e.* the handing over of suspected offenders who have been arrested in one jurisdiction for trial in the jurisdiction in which the alleged offence was committed, and extra-territorial jurisdiction, *i.e.* the trial in one jurisdiction of suspected offenders arrested in that jurisdiction for offences committed in another jurisdiction, and the position of the two Governments is discussed in detail in Chapter 4 below.

F: CROSS-BORDER CO-OPERATION ON SECURITY, ECONOMIC, SOCIAL AND CULTURAL MATTERS

Article 9

(*a*) With a view to enhancing cross-border co-operation on security matters, the Conference shall set in hand a programme of work to be undertaken by the Commissioner of the Garda Síochána and the Chief Constable of the Royal Ulster Constabulary and, where appropriate, groups of officials, in such areas as threat assessments, exchange of information, liaison structures, technical co-operation, training of personnel, and operational resources.

(*b*) The Conference shall have no operational responsibilities; responsibility for police operations shall remain with the heads of the respective police forces, the Commissioner of the Garda Síochána maintaining his links with the Minister for Justice and the Chief Constable of the Royal

Ulster Constabulary his links with the Secretary of State for Northern Ireland.

[This is the Irish version; in the British version precedence is given to British ministers and officials.]

GENERAL NOTE

Articles 9 and 10 deal with cross-border co-operation between Northern Ireland and the rest of Ireland on security and on other matters. There is a significant difference in the drafting of the two sets of provisions. Under Article 9 no reference is made to the possible devolution of responsibility for security to a Northern Ireland administration. The provisions of Article 10 in respect of other matters mirror the earlier provisions in respect of internal matters by providing that the Conference shall have jurisdiction only until agreement on devolution can be reached, upon which event alternative arrangements for cross-border co-operation between the Irish Government and a Northern Ireland administration would be established. In practical terms, however, it is unlikely that this difference could be sustained. If responsibility for security were to be devolved to a Northern Ireland administration, which is already provided for under the Northern Ireland Constitution Act 1973, the terms of Article 2(b) make it clear that the Conference would cease to have jurisdiction in that respect. In so far as direct co-operation between the British Army, in respect of which responsibility is unlikely to be devolved, and the Irish security forces might continue to be necessary, there might still be a role for the Conference in this respect, though it might be more appropriate for that to be subsumed in the framework of the Anglo-Irish Intergovernmental Council. But if the commitment by the Irish Government to the principle that the Irish Army should act only in support of the Garda Síochána were mirrored in Northern Ireland, even this continuing role for the Conference or Council might be effectively eliminated.

ANNOTATIONS

"With a view to enhancing cross-border co-operation on security matters, the Conference shall set in hand a programme of work to be undertaken by the Commissioner of the Garda Síochána and the Chief Constable of the Royal Ulster Constabulary and, where appropriate, groups of officials" This provision imposes an obligation on both police forces to set in hand a programme of work, rather than to implement any particular measures. In this respect it mirrors the general structure of the Agreement by providing for direct consultation and discussion between the Commissioner and the Chief Constable and their senior officers. This was a particularly important objective at the time when the Agreement was signed since it was widely known that relations between the two chiefs of police had become very strained. The programme of joint consultation at police level, however, is clearly set within the framework of the Conference. In practice the two chiefs of police have been expected to make regular reports on the progress of their joint working groups to full meetings of the Conference: see, for example, the communique of the 3rd meeting on January 10, 1986 at which the ministers stressed the urgency of rapid progress in this area and called for a progress report which was delivered at the 5th meeting on March 11, 1986. This pattern has been continued, with the two chiefs of police being asked to report to the Conference at most of its regular meetings, though their participation has usually been limited to that item on the agenda. No details of the content or the results of the programme of work have been published.

"in such areas as threat assessments, exchange of information, liaison structures" These three items cover much the same ground. In practice it appears to have been agreed that all communications and exchange of information, both on longer term intelligence and on immediate operational matters, should be channelled through the police system even where the information originates from or is of most direct relevance to army personnel. This is to emphasise the formal subordination of the two armies to the police.

"technical co-operation" This would appear to refer to possible co-operation in the choice of equipment and in forensic investigation; the absence of any public or official confrontation over the separate post mortem investigations by the two state pathologists of the body of Aidan McAnespie, who was shot dead at a border crossing on February 21, 1988 may be taken as an example both of the possibility and of the benefits from such co-operation, not least in dispelling suspicions that evidence is being manipulated or concealed on either side.

"training of personnel" It has been suggested on a number of occasions that there would be advantages in increasing links between the two police forces in Ireland by the development of specialist training courses in Ireland in which members of both forces might participate, rather than for the RUC to rely almost exclusively on facilities in Britain. It is not clear from reports of Conference meetings whether any positive action has been agreed under this heading.

41

"and operational resources" This suggests the possibility of some sharing of resources in manpower and physical facilities. One possibility which has been suggested on a number of occasions is that in certain border areas joint patrols might be arranged so that any difficulty in pursuing suspected offenders across the border might be minimised. To date political objections to any "incursion" by the RUC or the British Army into Irish territory and to a lesser extent by the Garda Síochána and the Irish Army into Northern Ireland have prevented any developments of this kind, though it has been reported that agreement was finally reached in 1988 on limited permission for aerial flights over Irish territory by British Army helicopters for surveillance purposes.

"The Conference shall have no operational responsibilities" This provision reflects the general principle set out in Article 2; unlike the provision which follows, it clearly applies both to police and to Army operations.

"responsibility for police operations shall remain with the heads of the respective police forces" This provision emphasises the constitutional position in both the United Kingdom and Ireland that operational control of policing rests with the head of the police force subject only to whatever directions may be given under an express statutory provision and to general control by the courts of the abuse or non-use of a statutory or common law power. In Northern Ireland, for example, certain orders in respect of the banning as opposed to the re-routeing of marches and demonstrations can only be made by the Secretary of State on the advice of the Chief Constable: see Public Order (Northern Ireland) Order 1986, arts. 3 to 5. The common law in this respect in Britain is set out in *R. v. Metropolitan Police Commissioner, ex p. Blackburn* [1968] 2 Q.B. 118. In both jurisdictions, however, this is separate from the issue of appointment and dismissal (see below).

"the Commissioner of the Garda Síochána maintaining his links with the Minister for Justice" Under section 6 of the Police Forces Amalgamation Act 1925 the Commissioner of the Garda Síochána is appointed by and may at any time be removed by the Government, though it has been held that this does not absolve the Government from adopting fair procedures in so doing (*Garvey* v. *Ireland* [1981] I.R. 75); otherwise the Commissioner has a similar operational discretion to that of the chief constable in British law. There is no police authority in Ireland, though the idea was proposed by the Coalition Government which signed the Agreement.

"and the Chief Constable of the Royal Ulster Constabulary his links with the Secretary of State for Northern Ireland" In formal terms the Chief Constable is appointed by and may be dismissed by the Police Authority for Northern Ireland, which also has the statutory responsibility for securing the maintenance of an adequate and efficient police force in Northern Ireland (Police Act (Northern Ireland) 1970, ss.1 and 7). The members of the Police Authority are appointed by the Secretary of State for Northern Ireland and may be removed before the expiry of their term of office only if unfit to continue or incapable of performing their duties (*ibid.*, Sched. 1). Thus there is no direct control by the Secretary of State over either the Police Authority or the Chief Constable, though certain powers under the Public Order (Northern Ireland) Order in relation to the banning of parades or meetings can be exercised only by the Secretary of State on the advice of the Chief Constable (see above). Nor can the Police Authority give any binding instructions to the Chief Constable on the performance of his statutory and common law duties. The constitutional position of the Chief Constable as an independent office holder subject only to the courts is the same as that of chief constables in Britain: see *R. v. Metropolitan Police Commissioner, ex p. Blackburn* [1968] 2 Q.B. 118 and *R. v. Secretary of State for the Home Department, ex p. Northumbria Police Authority* [1988] 2 W.L.R. 590. The links referred to in this provision must be taken to refer to the regular security meetings held by the Secretary of State with the Chief Constable and the General Officer Commanding the British Army in Northern Ireland.

Article 10

(a) The two Governments shall co-operate to promote the economic and social development of those areas of both parts of Ireland which have suffered most severely from the consequences of the instability of recent years, and shall consider the possibility of securing international support for this work.

(b) If it should prove impossible to achieve and sustain devolution on a basis which secures widespread acceptance in Northern Ireland, the Conference shall be a framework for the promotion of co-operation between the two parts of Ireland concerning cross-border aspects of economic, social and cultural matters in relation to which the Secretary of State for Northern Ireland continues to exercise authority.

(*c*) If responsibility is devolved in respect of certain matters in the economic, social or cultural areas currently within the responsibility of the Secretary of State for Northern Ireland, machinery will need to be established by the responsible authorities in the North and South for practical co-operation in respect of cross-border aspects of these issues.

ANNOTATIONS

"The two Governments shall co-operate to promote the economic and social development of those areas of both parts of Ireland which have suffered most severely from the consequences of the instability of recent years" This provision is more limited than that of the following paragraphs, in that it refers to economic and social but not cultural development and in that it is limited to areas which have suffered most severely from the "Troubles." The relevant areas have in practice been defined as all six counties of Northern Ireland and the adjacent border counties of Ireland, *i.e.* Donegal, Leitrim, Cavan, Monaghan and Louth with the addition of Sligo. This choice, including the somewhat anomalous addition of County Sligo, appears to have been made to keep in line with the area designated for special cross-border aid by the European Commission. As indicated in the commentary on the International Fund (see below), the area could readily be either extended or further limited on either side of the border since there is no clear guidance as to how "most severe suffering" should be measured. It does not appear that any action has been taken under this provision apart from that in respect of the International Fund, though if international support were to be phased out the two Governments would still be under an obligation to continue to co-operate in pursuit of the same objectives.

"and shall consider the possibility of securing international support for this work" This is an indirect reference to the International Fund for Ireland which was planned as a means both of emphasising international support for the Agreement and of encouraging popular support for it in both parts of Ireland. Though formal reference to possible international financial support was made only at the 1st meeting of the Conference on December 11, 1985 diplomatic efforts to procure it continued throughout 1985 and 1986. As explained in detail in Chapter 3 below, a formal agreement to establish the International Fund was entered into by the British and Irish Governments on September 18, 1986 as soon as financial support from the United States had finally been assured. Further contributions have since been made by Canada and New Zealand and further support from the European Commission was reported at the 22nd meeting of the Conference on June 17, 1988. The working of the Fund was reviewed at the 23rd meeting on July 27, 1988 at which it was agreed that the views of the two Governments on future direction and priorities should be conveyed to the Board of the Fund. The response of the Board and the general working of the Fund is also discussed in Chapter 3 below.

"If it should prove impossible to achieve and sustain devolution on a basis which secures widespread acceptance in Northern Ireland, the Conference shall be a framework" The wording is identical to that of Article 5(c) in respect of political matters; for a discussion of the general issue of devolution see the commentary on Article 4, in which the words "on a basis which would secure widespread acceptance throughout the community" are used.

"For the promotion of co-operation between the two parts of Ireland concerning cross-border aspects of economic, social and cultural matters" This provision, as already noted, is wider than that in paragraph (a) in that it is not restricted to areas which have suffered most severely from the "Troubles" and in that it extends to cultural matters. On the other hand it is explicitly limited to matters involving cross-border co-operation. An illustrative list of matters was published following the 5th meeting of the Conference on March 11, 1986:

CROSS-BORDER SOCIAL AND ECONOMIC CO-OPERATION

1. Economic

Tourism	— regular contact on various projects
Youth Training	— cross-border exchanges of trainees
EC-Associated Joint Training Projects	— various projects supported by the European Social Fund
Industrial Science Co-operation	— joint compilation of directories of expertise and services, by Co-operation North
Marketing	— joint participation in industrial promotions/exhibitions
Industrial Relations	— mutual exchange of industrial relations experience

Employment Equality	— regular contact on common issues
Petroleum Exploration	— exchange of information on exploration in areas straddling the border
National Economic and Social Council/Northern Ireland Economic Council	— co-operation on matters of mutual interest
Industrial Design	— joint co-operation

2. Infrastructure and Services

Newry/Dundalk Road	— joint consideration of improved road links
Water Services	— reciprocal arrangements on water services in border areas

3. Transport

Freight Haulage Licensing	— licensing of cross-border hauliers
Motor Vehicle Administration	— general liaison in relation to motor vehicle registration
Transport Companies	— regular contacts on road and rail issues of mutual interest
Commissioners of Irish Lights	— maintenance of lights and navigational aids
Marine Search and Rescue	— operational liaison and co-operation
Road Safety	— regular contacts

4. Agriculture and Fisheries

Trade in Agricultural Produce	— co-operation on trade and EC funds including abuses
Animal, Plant and Fish Health	— co-operation to maintain/improve disease status
Drainage	— co-ordination of complementary programmes
Foyle Fisheries Commission	— joint administration of Foyle Salmon Fisheries
Sea Fisheries	— discussions about fishing limits
Timber Utilisation	— exchanges of information on marketing and development
Horse Breeding and Racing	— joint administration of breeding scheme and regulation of racing

5. Health and Social Security

Medicines and Food Control	— co-operation of cross-border control
Availability of Health Services	— liaison in relation to the provision of health services
Medical Self-Certification of ESSP Scheme	— exchange of information and experience
Social Security Reform and Computerisation	— exchange of information and experience
Social Security Fraud	— co-operation on counter cross-border fraud
Health Board Co-operation in North West	— cross-border liaison on health services
Nuclear Radiation	— exchange of information and regular liaison
Infectious and Contagious Diseases	— exchange of information and concerted action
Medical and Dental Manpower	— exchange of information on mutual manpower problems

6. Education

School Teachers and Inspector Exchanges	— regular exchanges
Higher Education	— co-operation between Higher Education Institutions
Teacher Qualifications	— consideration of reciprocal recognition
Museums, Libraries and Films	— regular exchanges
Youth Affairs	— co-operation in youth exchanges
History Seminars for Teachers	— joint educational seminars
European Studies (Ireland)	— shared curriculum development

7. Environmental

Environmental Protection	— joint meetings on pollution, water quality, *etc.*
Planning	— joint co-operation on issues straddling the border
Conservation	— joint ecological considerations
Historic Monuments and Buildings	— joint contact on archaeology and historic buildings

8. Taxation

Inland Revenue	— operational contacts
Enforcement of Revenue Matters	— operational contacts
Customs Procedures and Documentation	— operational contacts

9. Joint Studies

EC-Assisted Cross-Border Studies	— joint studies supported by the European Regional Development Fund
Lough Melvin Study	— joint consideration of environmental study
North/West Study	— joint consideration of proposals by an independent study group

10. Arts, Sport and Cultural

Sport	— development of cross-border co-operation on sporting activities
Voluntary Organisations in Community Relations	— wide range of bodies supported by both Governments
Arts Councils Co-operation	— frequent exchanges and practical co-operation
Public Records	— links at official and university levels on historical record matters

11. Miscellaneous

District Council Contacts	— regular contacts on matters of mutual interest in border areas
Fire and Emergency Services	— operational liaison in cross-border areas
Natural Disaster Contingency Planning	— exchange of information
Ordnance Surveys	— contacts on mutual survey problems and joint publication
Metereological Service	— operational liaison
General Register Office	— liaison in relation to registration of births, deaths and marriages and other census matters
Irish Soldiers and Sailors Land Trust	— co-operation on the Trust and its future
Training Conferences	— joint conferences/visits between public service training centres

It would appear that much of the activity on these matters has taken place at official level. Discussions on tourism were reported at the 6th meeting of the Conference on May 9, 1986 and on the Newry-Dundalk road at the 7th and 9th meetings on June 17, 1986 and October 6, 1986. A general review was submitted at the 14th meeting on April 22, 1987 which included specific reference to the desirability of separate meetings by the responsible ministers on either side on particular items and also to a proposed study on the development of employment opportunities in the North-West. Further bilateral ministerial meetings on health and economic matters were reported at the 22nd and 23rd meetings on June 17, 1988 and July 27, 1988.

"in relation to which the Secretary of State for Northern Ireland continues to exercise authority" A similar phrase is used in Article 5(c). The intention appears to be to limit the jurisdiction of the Conference to matters dealt with on a purely Northern Ireland basis, thus excluding those which fall under the jurisdiction of the Anglo-Irish Intergovernmental Council. In distinction to the provisions of Article 5(c), there is no reference to the further restriction to "matters within the purview of the Northern Ireland Departments."

"If responsibility is devolved in respect of certain matters in the economic, social or cultural areas currently within the responsibility of the Secretary of State for Northern Ireland" This formulation mirrors that of paragraph (b), though it recognises that responsibility might be devolved on some but not all these matters.

"machinery will need to be established by the responsible authorities in the North and South" This provision merely states that such machinery will be needed, since under the general structure of the Agreement the Conference is to cease to have jurisdiction over devolved matters. It does not impose any obligation on either Government to ensure that it is provided or even in respect of the Irish Government to co-operate in establishing it. The omission in

respect of the British Government is a recognition of the fact that the Agreement could not bind any future devolved administration in Northern Ireland; it is surprising that no attempt was made to bind the Irish Government to co-operate in any such structure. The main unionist parties in Northern Ireland have repeatedly stressed that they would wish to co-operate with the Irish Government on such matters provided that all territorial and jurisdictional claims by the Irish Government over Northern Ireland are removed: see, for example, the submission of the Democratic Unionist Party to the Devolution Report Committee of the Northern Ireland Assembly (First Report, Northern Ireland Assembly 154, Appendix B (October 1984)) and the open letter addressed to the Prime Minister by the two Unionist leaders, James Molyneaux and Ian Paisley, on August 28, 1985. The use of the words "responsible authorities" probably reflects the desire of the drafters to avoid any commitment as to the form or name of a devolved administration in Northern Ireland and perhaps also not to eliminate the possibility of some form of federal relationship in a New Ireland of the kind considered in the *New Ireland Forum Report*. The use of the words "North and South" probably reflects similar concerns to avoid specific commitment on these matters.

"for practical co-operation in respect of cross-border aspects of these issues" This formulation, like that in paragraph (b), emphasises that only cross-border aspects are envisaged. The word "practical," which does not appear in paragraph (b), may have been inserted to emphasise that no constitutional implications were intended.

G: Arrangements for Review

Article 11

At the end of three years from signature of this Agreement, or earlier if requested by either Government, the working of the Conference shall be reviewed by the two Governments to see whether any changes in the scope and nature of its activities are desirable.

General Note

The intention of this Article was to provide for a general review of the working of the Conference at the end of a specified period. The provisions of Article 1 of the Agreement were intentionally excluded from the review on the ground that they were supposed to provide reassurance to unionists by entrenching the recognition of the constitutional status of Northern Ireland. As indicated in the Introduction and in the commentary on Article 1, however, this is of limited significance in law, since the terms of Article 1 were carefully drafted to avoid any constitutional implications and since any part of the Agreement can in any event be altered at any time with the agreement of both sides. In addition, the precise nature of the review is not spelled out, leaving it open to the two Governments to adopt either a minimalist position, under which they would merely review the practical working of the Conference without considering any amendments to the wording of the Agreement, or a more general review which would include consideration of possible changes to the Agreement itself. Any such changes in wording, as indicated in the Introduction, could be adopted with the consent of both sides either by way of an additional protocol to the Agreement or by way of a new Agreement to supersede the existing one. Though it initially appeared to be the intention of the two Governments to adopt a minimalist position, it has been announced by the Secretary of State for Northern Ireland that the "review . . . will examine the whole working of the Conference and its associated Secretariat to see whether any changes in the scope and nature of its activities are desirable" (Press Statement, October 21, 1988) and that the views of all interested parties will be taken into account (Press Statement, October 11, 1988). At the 25th meeting of the Conference on November 2, 1988 it was agreed that "a thorough and serious review of the working of the Conference under each of the articles of the Agreement" should be undertaken with the main emphasis on a positive programme to further its aims. (The Review was finally completed and published on May 24, 1989; it is reproduced without further commentary in Chapter 7.)

Annotations

"At the end of three years from signature of this Agreement, or earlier if requested by either Government" In the absence of any request for a prior review by either side, the review is to

46

begin on November 15, 1988; though no provision is made for the termination of the review it was agreed at the 25th meeting of the Conference on November 2, 1988 that it was envisaged that it would be completed by early 1989.

"the working of the Conference shall be reviewed by the two Governments" This formulation suggests a limited review of the working of the Conference rather than the terms of the Agreement and that the review might be limited to the two Governments, thus excluding or at least not encouraging submissions from other interested parties. As noted above, the two Governments have decided on a broader and more open review.

"to see whether any changes in the scope and nature of its activities are desirable" This formulation suggests a wider review of the terms of the Agreement under which the Conference operates, since if the scope or nature of its activities is to be extended or restricted some change in the relevant Articles, or at least in those which impose mandatory obligations, would be required. No official acknowledgement has yet been made of the possibility of changes in the wording of the Agreement following the review.

H: INTERPARLIAMENTARY RELATIONS

Article 12

It will be for Parliamentary decision in Dublin and in Westminster whether to establish an Anglo-Irish Parliamentary body of the kind adumbrated in the Anglo-Irish Studies Report of November 1981. The two Governments agree that they would give support as appropriate to such a body, if it were to be established.

GENERAL NOTE

The idea of creating a parliamentary tier for the new structures for Anglo-Irish relations to complement the work of the Anglo-Irish Intergovernmental Council and Conference may be traced directly to the Anglo-Irish Studies of 1981, which suggested that the existing Anglo-Irish Parliamentary Group might be developed into a more formal body with the participation of members of the Northern Ireland Assembly as well as of the Parliaments in London and Dublin (Cmnd. 8414, paras. 14 to 18; Pl. 299, paras. 14 to 18). Following the completion of the Anglo-Irish Studies in 1981 it was agreed at the summit meeting between Mrs Thatcher and Dr Fitzgerald on November 6, 1981 that the British and Irish Parliaments might consider at an appropriate time "whether there should be an Anglo-Irish body at parliamentary level comprising members to be drawn from the British and Irish Parliaments, the European Parliament and any elected assembly that may be established for Northern Ireland". The possibility of such a body has been raised from time to time in both Parliaments, most recently by a group of six British and Irish politicians lead by Peter Temple-Morris MP and Jim Tunney TD. This plan, which has been submitted in the form of a joint Working Paper for approval by the two Governments, envisages the establishment of a body consisting of 50 members drawn in equal numbers from the two Parliaments and including representatives from the largest parties in Northern Ireland, the established parties in Britain and each of the parties in the Dáil. This body would meet twice yearly to discuss matters of mutual interest. Presumably in an effort to secure unionist support, the originators of the plan have been careful not to link it directly with Article 12 of the Agreement (*Irish Times*, November 2, 1988).

It may be noted that a similar parliamentary tier to that described in the Anglo-Irish Studies was envisaged for the Council of Ireland proposed at the Sunningdale Conference: this body was to have both a Council of Ministers drawn from the Irish Government and the Northern Ireland Executive and a Consultative Assembly composed of 30 members each from Dáil Éireann and the Northern Ireland Assembly (Communique, para. 7). The Council of Ireland provided for in the Government of Ireland Act 1920, however, was to be composed only of members of the Parliaments of Northern Ireland and Southern Ireland, though it was to have both legislative and executive powers on certain cross-border matters (ss.2 and 10). Neither of these bodies was ever established. The best example of an international parliamentary body with effective powers is the Nordic Council which was established in 1953 with representatives of the paraliaments of Denmark, Norway, Sweden, Finland and Iceland and which since 1971 has had a Council of Ministers with limited powers to take decisions by unanimity. Comparison may also be made with the parliamentary tiers of the Council of Europe and the European Community. In every case, however, the success of such a body is likely to depend on the creation of a useful and effective role for it. The precise function of an Anglo-Irish Interparliamentary body has never been made clear. One possibility would be for

The Anglo-Irish Agreement

it to monitor the progress of the Agreement or the workings of the Anglo-Irish Intergovernmental Council and Conference, with specialist select committees with powers to question ministers and officials from both sides on their achievements and plans.

ANNOTATIONS

"It will be for Parliamentary decision in Dublin and in Westminster whether to establish an Anglo-Irish Parliamentary body of the kind adumbrated in the Anglo-Irish Studies Report of November 1981" This provision preserves the constitutional proprieties on both sides by making it clear that it is for the respective Parliaments to decide on the creation of a parliamentary tier. It may be questioned, given the current practice in both Parliaments for most decisions to be determined in advance by the Government and pressed through by party whips, whether it is entirely realistic for the initiative to be left to the Parliaments. The suggestions in the Anglo-Irish Studies Report (Cmnd. 8414; Pl. 299) are summarised in the Introduction (above).

"The two Governments agree that they would give support as appropriate to such a body, if it were to be established" This cautiously drafted provision does not commit the Governments to supporting any particular form of interparliamentary body.

I: FINAL CLAUSES

Article 13

This Agreement shall enter into force on the date on which the two Governments exchange notifictions of their acceptance of this Agreement.

GENERAL NOTE

Notifications were exchanged on November 29, 1985 immediately following the registration of the Agreement at the United Nations.

In witness whereof the undersigned, being duly authorised thereto by their respective Governments, have signed this Agreement.

Done in two originals at Hillsborough on the 15th day of November 1985.

For the Government of the United Kingdom of Great Britain and Northern Ireland, Margaret Thatcher.

For the Government of the Republic of Ireland, Gearóid Mac Gearailt (British version).

For the Government of Ireland, Gearóid Mac Gearailt.

For the Government of the United Kingdom, Margaret Thatcher (Irish version).

GENERAL NOTE

The signature of two originals, each describing the two Governments in different ways, is discussed in the commentary on the Preamble.

CHAPTER 3

THE INTERNATIONAL FUND FOR IRELAND

Introductory note

The International Fund for Ireland was established by the British and Irish Governments to co-ordinate international expressions of financial support made after the signing of the Anglo-Irish Agreement and to further the aims envisaged therein. It has its basis in Article 10(a) of the Agreement which states:

"The two Governments shall co-operate to promote the economic and social development of those areas of both parts of Ireland which have suffered most severely from the consequences of the instability of recent years, and shall consider the possibility of securing inter-national support for this work."

On September 18, 1986 the two Governments concluded a formal inter-state agreement (see below) which provided for the setting up of the Inter-national Fund for Ireland. This was subsequently ratified by the British and Irish Parliaments and came into force on December 12, 1986. As at September 30, 1988 three countries had made donations to the Fund: the USA, Canada and New Zealand. The United States aid-package was approved by Congress on September 19, 1986 with the passing of the Anglo-Irish Agreement Support Act and carried into effect under the terms of the *Agreement between the Government of Ireland, the Government of the United Kingdom of Great Britain and Northern Ireland and the Government of the United States of America concerning the International Fund for Ireland* (Cmnd. 9910), signed in Washington on September 26, 1986. To date the USA has made a grant of US$120 million, the third payment of which was received by the Fund in September 1988. There are also proposals for a fourth contribution from the USA in 1989. Canada, in an *Agreement between the Government of Canada and the International Fund for Ireland regarding a contribution by Canada to the Fund*, has made a first payment of Can$1.5 million and promised additional payments of up to Can$8.5 million over ten years. New Zealand has provided NZ$300,000 as a single donation. As at September 30, 1988 the total available to the Fund for disbursement was equivalent to approximately UK£80 million. The terms under which each country has agreed to make a contribution are considered below. In 1989 the European Community will join the list of contributors by making a grant of 15 million ECUs followed by proposed payments of a similar amount in 1990 and 1991.

The Fund is administered by a seven-member Board which operates on a part-time basis and has been jointly appointed by the British and Irish Governments. The Chairman is Mr. Charles Brett. Meetings are attended by observers nominated by the donor Governments, with the right to speak but not to vote. The Board is supported by an Advisory Committee consisting of eight senior British and Irish civil servants; the day-to-day administration of the Fund is in the hands of two Directors-General based in Belfast and Dublin (see the annotation of Article 10 below).

By September 1988 the Board had implemented seven major programmes of work. Two venture capital companies have been established pursuant to Article 9 of the Agreement to establish the Fund (see below). A Business Enterprise Programme, referred to in Article 3 of the 1986 Agreement, has been devised with the aim of stimulating job creation initiatives, principally in smaller firms, in conjunction with Government industrial promotion agencies or local community groups. In the area of tourism, the Fund has supported improvements to existing accommodation amenities and the stimulation of new hotel building by the private sector in Northern Ireland. Resources have also been made available for the promotion of Ireland overseas. The importance of inner-city urban development is recognised in the commitment of UK£11 million to development programmes in 24 District Towns in Northern Ireland and 12 towns in the border areas of Ireland; the objective is to stimulate private investment in the 36 commercial centres which have been targeted for aid. Agriculture and fisheries has been allocated a budget of UK£4.329 million, the largest proportion of which is to be spent on farm diversification and fisheries development including marine research. In the area of science and technology UK£7.182 million has been made available to encourage innovation and the improvement of technological facilities in Northern Ireland, and to support cross-border technological co-operation and technology based economic development in the Border Regions. Finally, a Wider Horizons programme has been devised in accordance with Article 4(d) of the Agreement to establish the Fund (see below).

In September 1988 the Board, in consultation with the British and Irish Governments, reviewed its priorities and policies and decided that "a new, more focused contribution should be made to the economic and social regeneration of Northern Ireland, particularly the most disadvantaged areas, and of the six border counties in the South" (Press Statement, September 8, 1988). Priority was to be given to the most disadvantaged areas in three ways: firstly, through its existing programmes; secondly, through a special budget allocation of UK£3 million for a proposed Community Economic Regeneration scheme; and thirdly, through a further UK£3 million reserved for possible special projects in those areas which might not satisfy all the criteria required by its existing programmes. It is the intention of the Board to invest not less than 50 per cent. of its resources in disadvantaged areas.

The Board also resolved to embark upon a modest experimental venture into the field of community relations, both cross-border and cross-community. At the same time, in response to the wishes expressed by the two Governments, the Board undertook to carry out detailed appraisals and feasibility studies of "flagship" projects such as the re-opening of the Ballinamore/Ballyconnell Canal and a major tourist facility at Eamhain Macha/Navan Fort. These measures were welcomed by the British and Irish Governments at the meeting of the Intergovernmental Conference held in Dublin on September 13, 1988.

In attempting to comply with Article 10(a) of the Anglo-Irish Agreement, and the requirement that support be given to "those parts of Ireland which have suffered most severely from the consequences of the instability of recent years," the Governments through the Advisory Committee have indicated their wish that the Fund should interpret its remit in Ireland as comprising the six southern "border" counties, as identified for EC regional purposes, of Donegal, Sligo, Leitrim, Cavan, Monaghan and Louth and in Northern Ireland as all six counties of Northern Ireland (see the annotation of Article 9 below). The total population of this large area is around two million people, about 1.5 million in Northern Ireland and 0.5 million in the rest of Ireland. The Fund is enjoined to spend approximately three-quarters of its resources in Northern Ireland and approximately one-quarter in the rest of Ireland. In the disbursement of these resources, the Board is strongly committed to the principle of leverage, *i.e.* the principle that for every pound it contributes to a scheme, several more pounds will be contributed by others. Particular care is also taken to avoid substituting Fund resources for those already available from other sources in the public or private sectors. To date £26.579 million has been offered to 858 projects. It is estimated that these projects will create around 4,500 permanent full-time jobs, 4,000 construction jobs of varying duration and some additional part-time or seasonable jobs; and that they should underpin employment for 1,500 people in rural areas who might otherwise be forced to emigrate.

Annotation of Agreement

Agreement between the Government of the United Kingdom of Great Britain and Northern Ireland and the Government of the Republic of Ireland concerning the International Fund for Ireland

The Government of the United Kingdom of Great Britain and Northern Ireland and the Government of the Republic of Ireland: (British version)

Agreement between the Government of Ireland and the Government of the United Kingdom concerning the International Fund for Ireland

The Government of Ireland and the Government of the United Kingdom: (Irish version)

Desiring to establish a Fund to contribute to the work envisaged in Article 10(a) of the Anglo-Irish Agreement of 15 November 1985, which provides as follows: "The two Governments shall co-operate to promote the economic and social development of those areas of both parts of Ireland which have suffered most severely from the consequences of the instability of recent years, and shall consider the possibility of securing international support for this work."

Convinced that such a Fund would be an important expression of international support for the common commitment of the two Governments to peace, stability, dialogue and reconciliation in Ireland and their common opposition to the exploitation of instability for political ends;

Recognising that serious under-employment and multiple deprivation create an environment in which instability can flourish, and that instability and conflict in turn create conditions which are inimical to social and economic progress;

Recognising the damage caused to both parts of Ireland by that instability;

Have agreed as follows:

Article 1

The International Fund for Ireland is hereby established by the two Governments for the purposes and in the manner set out in this Agreement.

Article 2

The objectives of the Fund are to promote economic and social advance and to encourage contact, dialogue and reconciliation between nationalists and unionists throughout Ireland.

GENERAL NOTE

This section provides a concise statement of the Fund's objectives and makes it clear that they are to be pursued on an all-Ireland basis. In practice, however, these objectives are qualified by the clear onus placed on the Board to have regard to the wishes expressed by donors to the Fund. The USA has stated that its contributions should be used to stimulate new investment, job creation and economic reconstruction (Anglo-Irish Agreement Support Act 1986, s.6(2)). Canada has expressed the wish that its contribution should be used to finance a Youth Training and Exchange Programme, and for business co-operation (Agreement between the Government of Canada and the International Fund for Ireland regarding a contribution by Canada to the Fund, Art. II). New Zealand is content that its contribution should go into the common pool.

Article 3

In pursuance of these objectives, the Fund shall stimulate private investment and enterprise, supplement public programmes and encourage voluntary effort, including self-help schemes. In the voluntary sphere, special emphasis shall be placed on supporting economic and social projects sponsored by men and women of good will throughout Ireland who are engaged in the task of communal reconciliation. The need to maximise the economic and social benefits of the Fund in Ireland shall be an overriding consideration in making disbursements from its resources and these disbursements shall be consistent with the economic and social policies and priorities of the respective Governments. Because of the special problems in Northern Ireland associated with the instability of recent years, approximately three-quarters of the resources of the Fund shall be spent there.

GENERAL NOTE

This section elaborates further on the objectives of the Fund as set out in Article 2. It is stated that resources shall be devoted to stimulating private investment and enterprise, supplementing public programmes and encouraging voluntary effort, including self-help schemes. In accordance with this provision the Business Enterprise Programme has so far committed UK£8.347 million to job creation north and south of the border. Thus, for example, the Fund has part financed "Eurocentre West" in Derry; and the Townsend Enterprise Park, Westlink Enterprises, West Belfast Development Trust and Farset Enterprises Ltd., all in Belfast. In conformity with the wording of Article 3, the main elements of the Programme have been designed to complement the existing schemes and structures of the statutory agencies. For example, development officers have been appointed in local enterprise centres within Northern Ireland to open up new opportunities for local economic development. This arrangement is mirrored in Ireland by a small task force seeking to identify market opportunities and to find new methods of company collaboration locally.

In addition to the emphasis placed upon economic investment, Article 3 affords equal importance to the promotion of social projects geared towards communal reconciliation. However, because of the wishes expressed by donors (see annotation of Article 2 above), this has not been reflected in the disbursement profile of the Fund to date. Indeed, it would appear that the Fund has been constrained to concentrate its efforts on job creation almost to the exclusion of programmes directed towards communal reconciliation. In this respect it is instructive that funds have in general not been allocated to groups working to improve cross-border relations, or to museums, reading rooms and literary publications set up with these objectives in mind. The twin emphases of Article 3, development and reconciliation, will be discussed further in the conclusion.

The arrangement whereby three-quarters of the resources of the Fund are to be spent in Northern Ireland reflects the balance in the population between Northern Ireland (1.5 million) and the six "border" counties of Ireland (0.5 million).

Article 4

In accordance with the objectives and criteria set out above, the Fund shall give priority on a value for money basis to the following:

(a) the stimulation of private sector investment, in particular by means of venture capital arrangements using some of the resources of the Fund;

(b) projects of benefit to people in both parts of Ireland, for example, improved communications and greater co-operation in the economic, educational and research fields;

(c) projects to improve the quality and conditions of life for people in areas facing serious economic and/or social problems. Spending will be carefully targeted to meet needs arising from factors such as high unemployment, underdeveloped social, health or education facilities, poor environment and sub-standard infrastructures;

(d) projects to provide wider horizons for people from both traditions in Ireland including opportunities for industrial training and work experience overseas.

GENERAL NOTE

Article 4 details the expenditure priorities which must be observed by the Board of the International Fund. In this regard the inclusion of the phrase, "on a value for money basis," is a clear indication of the two Governments' eagerness to ensure that the resources provided by donor countries are invested in projects which will produce a worthwhile return.

The emphasis which subsection (a) places upon the stimulation of private sector investment is not only reflected in the Fund's Business Enterprise scheme, it is also a feature of a number of its other programmes of work. Thus, for example, one of the Board's declared objectives in the area of tourism is to encourage the private sector to build new hotels in specific areas where there is a particular shortage of hotel accommodation. Similarly, the Urban Development Programme is designed to lever private investment in the 36 towns identified. The reference to venture capital arrangements is a marker to the establishment of two Investment Companies north and south of the border. This is further elaborated upon in Article 9 below.

Subsection (b) enjoins the Board of the International Fund to give priority to projects of benefit to people in both parts of Ireland. In this regard there is particular reference to improved communications and greater co-operation in the economic, educational and research fields. Examples of projects supported by the Fund with these objectives in view include the decision of the Board in September 1988 to appraise the project for the re-opening of the Ballinamore-Ballyconnell canal, linking the River Erne with the River Shannon; support for the joint overseas marketing and sales promotion campaign for Irish goods launched as part of the Business Enterprise Programme; and the cross-border technological co-operation scheme which is designed to encourage research and product development as part of the Board's commitment to progress within the field of science and technology.

Subsection (c) stresses the importance of projects designed to improve the quality and conditions of life for people in areas facing serious economic and/or social problems. The emphasis placed upon the regeneration of disadvantaged areas has been recognised by the Board in its review of priorities and policies held in September 1988. Having emphasised the importance of disadvantaged areas, subsection (c) goes on to provide that expenditure within these localities should be designed to meet needs arising from factors such as high unemployment, underdeveloped social, health or education facilities, poor environment and sub-standard infrastructures. However, in the definition of disadvantaged areas for the purposes of the Fund's new programmes no specific reference has been made to subsection (c); instead the Board has adopted a formula which, according to the Fund's second annual report (at p. 36) reflects primarily unemployment rates, but also incorporates, to a lesser extent, other measurements of deprivation.

The fourth priority set out in Article 4 has led to the allocation of UK£6.5 million to a Wider Horizons Programme. This programme, a primary focus for Canada's contribution to the Fund (see Article III(a) of the Canadian Agreement with the Fund), is designed to encourage managers, workers and students from both sides of the border to learn new skills by practical work experience, training and education overseas. Thus, for example, UK£250,000 has been provided for a marketing training and work experience scheme for managers, craftsmen and apprentices at the Irish Institute for European Affairs in Louvain.

Article 5

(1) The Fund is established as an international organisation of which the two Governments are members.

(2) The Fund shall have legal personality. Its legal capacity shall include the capacity to contract, to acquire and dispose of property and to institute legal proceedings. In particular it shall have power to enter into agreements with any donor consistent with the provisions of this Agreement provided that neither Government has indicated any objection. The Fund shall be exempt from the payment of direct taxes.

GENERAL NOTE

Article 5(1) establishes the Fund as a unique international organisation with the two Governments as sole members. Paragraph (2) then states that the Fund shall have a separate legal personality with the capacity to contract, to acquire and dispose of property and to institute legal proceedings. The penultimate clause of paragraph (2) reserves a right of veto to the British and Irish Governments in respect of the Fund's power to enter into agreements with prospective donors. Legislation has been passed in the United Kingdom (The International Fund for Ireland (Immunities and Privileges) Order 1986) and Ireland (The International Fund for Ireland (Designation and Immunities) Order 1986) to exempt the Fund from direct taxation, but not from VAT. This exemption has been extended by administrative decision to IFI (Southern Investments) Ltd. but not to IFI (Northern Investments) Ltd.

Article 6

The Fund shall have as its sole principal organ a Board which will consist of a Chairman and not less than six other members. The Chairman and other members of the Board shall be appointed jointly by the two Governments. They shall serve on terms and conditions decided by the two Governments. Donor countries if they so wish may send observers to participate in Board meetings. The decisions of the Board shall be taken by a majority. The Board shall, subject to the approval of the two Governments, establish rules of procedure and operating rules. Under these rules, a power of the Board may be delegated to one or more of its members. Subject to this Agreement, the members of the Board shall act independently and shall not receive instructions from Governments as to the exercise of their powers.

GENERAL NOTE

Article 6 lays down certain rules relating to the composition and procedure of the Board administering the Fund. It is stated that the Board shall consist of six ordinary members and a Chairman appointed jointly and serving on terms and conditions decided by the two Governments. The right of donor countries to send observers to participate in Board meetings has been exercised extensively in the past two years: representatives of the United States, Canadian and New Zealand Governments have attended the meetings held by the Board since its establishment in September 1986. The remainder of Article 6 reserves to the Board a right of independent action subject to the approval by the two Governments of the Fund's mode of operation. Although they are crucial to the everyday working of the Fund, the terms of these rules have not been published.

Article 7

The Board shall consider applications for assistance from the resources of the Fund and, if the Board is satisfied that they fall within the purposes set out above, may authorise grants and loans to any authority or any person or association for the purposes set out in the foregoing articles. The Fund shall also provide resources for the establishment of the two companies referred to in Article 9 below.

GENERAL NOTE

Article 7 obliges the Board to consider applications for assistance from the resources of the Fund. At the end of the first accounting period—September 30, 1987—1,112 applications were in the course of appraisal. By the end of September 1988 the Board had processed the applications received to the point where 858 offers have been made, representing a total to date of UK£26,579,000. In addition to the requirement that applications fall within the purposes laid down in the Agreement to establish the Fund, it is clear that the Board must take care to meet obligations placed upon them by donors to the Fund. Thus, for example, the letter of offer issued to each successful applicant includes the requirement that any money allocated be used in a non-discriminatory manner (see Anglo-Irish Agreement Support Act, s.5(c)(2)(A)). Although the appraisal of projects is made partly through consultants and partly through existing public agencies, the procedure by which offers of financial support are made is monitored in every case by members of the Board. Whilst this section empowers the Fund to make loans, the largest proportion of the assistance provided so far has been in the form of grants.

The Article also requires the Fund to provide resources for the establishment of the two investment companies referred to in Article 9.

Article 8

The Fund may contribute to the resources of existing bodies specialising in the provision of venture capital to be used for purposes within Article 4 of this Agreement.

This provision empowers the Fund to contribute to the resources of companies specialising in the provision of venture capital for purposes falling within Article 4. To date this power has not been exercised.

Article 9

The Fund shall also provide money for and initiate the establishment of two Investment Companies, one to be established in each part of Ireland, with a significant number of common directors and similar objectives, whose function will be to furnish venture capital for the private sector. Persons of established commercial experience especially in the international field shall be invited by the Board of the Fund to participate in the management of these Companies. Each of these Companies shall be concerned with ventures primarily in one of the two parts of Ireland and shall be registered there: but in appropriate cases, they may both support a venture or enterprise. The Companies shall identify the risk capital needs for ventures of existing or new industrial and commercial enterprises and will provide, on sound commercial criteria, equity capital or loans. The aim of the Companies shall be further to stimulate viable and self-sustaining growth in the private sector of the economies of both parts of Ireland.

GENERAL NOTE

IFI (Northern) Investments Ltd. and IFI (Southern) Investments Ltd. are the two venture capital companies established in accordance with this provision. The objects of the two companies are identical and include the promotion of the aims of the International Fund by providing equity capital and loans for commercial projects and investment. Each of these companies has a share capital of £5 million which is fully paid up. The Board of the Fund has emphasised the need for this capital to be self-regenerating. Thus, only projects with long-term profitability and real commercial potential have been supported.

IFI (Northern) Investments Ltd. was incorporated on September 8, 1987 and has its headquarters at Bulloch House, Linenhall Street, Belfast 2. Investments in two projects have so far been agreed. An investment of UK£254,000 has been made in Neotech Industries International Inc., a United States manufacturer of micro-electronic pressure gauges which has established a wholly-owned subsidiary in the Antrim Technology Park. It is envisaged that this project will result in the direct employment of some 200 people. A second equity investment of UK£22,000 has been made in Portavogie Boatyard which offers a repair and re-engining facility to the local fishing fleet and other boat owners. It is reported (see the Fund's Second Annual Report at p. 8) that the Board of IFI (Northern) Investments Ltd. has approved in principle investments in and is finalising investment agreements with five other companies involving a proposed total commitment of a further £1,350,000.

IFI (Southern) Investments Ltd., incorporated on September 17, 1987 and based in Dundalk, has so far considered 85 proposals. Decisions have been taken to invest IR£800,000 in three of the projects submitted, although investment agreements had not been finally concluded before the end of the Fund's second accounting period—September 30, 1988. It is reported (see Second Annual Report at p. 9) that 18 further proposals are under active consideration, involving total investments of IR£2.5 million. The three approved projects are expected to result directly or indirectly in the employment of approximately 800 people.

The directors of the two companies are appointed by the Fund and comprise a total of 12 individuals, three of whom act as common directors and four of whom also serve on the Board of the International Fund itself (see para. 11, Articles of Association, IFI (Northern) Investments Ltd. and para. 21, Articles of Association, IFI (Southern) Investments Ltd.). The Chairman of IFI (Northern) Investments Ltd. is W. Carson, FCA, former senior partner, Price Waterhouse, Belfast; his southern counterpart is D. McGuane, formerly of W. & R. Jacob PLC. In common with the Board of the International Fund, the Directors of IFI (Southern) Investments Ltd. have so far interpreted their geographical remit as being strictly limited to the six border counties of Cavan, Donegal, Leitrim, Louth, Monaghan and Sligo. This is despite the fact that no such restriction appears either in the Memorandum and Articles of Association upon which it was incorporated or in the Agreement to establish the Fund; indeed, Articles 2 and 3 of that Agreement enjoin the Board to pursue the objectives for which it was established "throughout Ireland."

The Anglo-Irish Agreement

Article 10

The Board shall be assisted by an Advisory Committee composed of representatives of the two Governments, in particular as regards all applications made to the Fund under Article 7. The accommodation and secretarial services necessary for the proper functioning of the Fund, together with its general administrative and organisational expenses, shall be provided jointly by the two Governments.

GENERAL NOTE

The Advisory Committee referred to in Article 10 has been established to assist the Board, particularly in respect of the appraisal of all applications for assistance made under Article 7. This Committee comprises eight senior civil servants, four each appointed by the British and Irish Governments. The day-to-day administration of the Fund is entrusted to two Joint Directors-General, Mr. A. I. Devitt (Belfast) and Mr. B. J. Lyons (Dublin), whose services and those of small supporting groups in Belfast and Dublin are made available by the civil service departments to which they belong. The Fund has no staff or premises of its own and as a matter of policy the Board itself does not meet on government property.

In addition to the work of the Advisory Committee, "the board has delegated to specialist agencies, including some Government Departments, responsibility for the administration of its various programmes within criteria and operating arrangements specified by the board. The activities of administering agencies in respect of their responsibilities for fund programmes are closely monitored by the board" (H.C. Deb. col. 444w (March 14, 1988)).

Article 11

The Board shall appoint auditors who will annually audit the accounts of the Fund. The report of the auditors shall be published.

GENERAL NOTE

Coopers & Lybrand, auditors to the International Fund, published their first report on December 6, 1987 and their second report on December 2, 1988.

Article 12

The Board shall present annually a report to the two Governments and to donors to the Fund.

GENERAL NOTE

The Fund's first annual report was published on December 10, 1987 and its second annual report was published on December 15, 1988. Both were presented by the Board to the Government of the United Kingdom, the Government of Ireland and the Governments of the donor countries in accordance with this provision. A progress report was published after the 12th meeting of the Board on April 8, 1988.

Article 13

This Agreement may be amended by a further Agreement between the two Governments.

GENERAL NOTE

Article 13 states that the Agreement to establish the Fund may be amended by a further Agreement between the two Governments. This provision amounts to a formal statement of the power to vary an agreement which is already available under the international law of treaties. To date no amendment has been made to the Agreement to establish the Fund.

Article 14

This Agreement shall enter into force on the date on which the two Governments exchange notifications of their acceptance of it except that Article 5(2) shall become effective only after the completion of any remaining steps necessary in that connection. The Agreement shall continue in force until terminated by mutual agreement or by one Government giving the other six months' written notice, and thereafter shall remain in force for as long as and to the extent necessary for an orderly disposal of any remaining assets of the Fund in accordance with the spirit of the Agreement in full consultation with the donors.

In witness whereof the undersigned, being duly authorised thereto by their respective Governments, having signed this Agreement.

Done in two originals at both Dublin and London on the 18th day of September 1986.

For the Government of Ireland, Paedar de Borra

For the Government of the United Kingdom, R. F. Stimson (Irish version)

Done in two originals at both London and Dublin on the 18th day of September 1986.

For the Government of the United Kingdom of Great Britain and Northern Ireland, Geoffrey Howe

For the Government of the Republic of Ireland, Noel Dorr (British version)

GENERAL NOTE

Article 14 details formal arrangements for the Agreement's entry into force and the possible repudiation of it either by mutual consent or a unilateral declaration. On September 18, 1986 two originals of the Agreement were signed in both London and Dublin by representatives of the two Governments in the presence of the United States and Canadian Ambassadors. Like the Anglo-Irish Agreement, there are some differences in the descriptions of the parties to the Agreement to establish the Fund. However, the operative terms of the Treaty are similar in both the British and Irish versions. The two Governments exchanged notifications of their acceptance of the Treaty in Dublin on December 1, 1986, and Article 5(2) became effective on December 12, 1986 when the Fund legally came into existence.

Conclusion

The progress of the International Fund to date can be divided into two specific phases. For the first two years of its existence the Fund sought "to effect a lasting and coherent improvement in the economic climate of the northern counties of Ireland as a whole" (C. E. B. Brett, Second Annual Report at p. 4) through the dispersal of monies to a large number of smaller projects based over a wide area. Then in September 1988, the Board honed its existing programmes and developed new ones because it was felt that "a more focused contribution should be made to the economic and social regeneration of the most disadvantaged areas" (C. E. B. Brett, Second Annual Report at p. 4). Thus, the Fund has now resolved to concentrate its efforts on projects located in those areas where the need is perceived to be greatest.

It seems likely that this change of policy has come at the prompting of the British and Irish Governments. At the 23rd meeting of the Anglo-Irish Intergovernmental Conference, held in London on July 27, 1988, the two Governments noted the importance of projects which the Fund had already supported in disadvantaged areas and "agreed that it was timely that the Board would shortly be considering its future strategy, and decided that they should convey to the Board the agreed views of the two Governments on the future direction and priorities of the Fund, having regard in particular to Article 10(a) of the Agreement."

Despite the review which took place in September, the twin emphases of

Article 10(a) of the Anglo-Irish Agreement and Article 3 of the Agreement to establish the Fund upon economic and social development has not been reflected in the Board's programmes and expenditure priorities to date. Thus, as indicated in the annotation of Article 3 above, the Fund has concentrated its efforts on job creation at the expense of programmes directed towards communal reconciliation. The Board of the Fund defines its approach as one of seeking to achieve "reconciliation through the promotion of private-sector prosperity and enhanced employment prospects" (C. E. B. Brett, April 1988 Progress Report at p. 5). Thus, it has actively discouraged applications for projects of a purely recreational, educational, cultural, charitable or suchlike nature (see April 1988 Progress Report at p. 5). Yet, it can be argued that, where reconciliation is the objective, the funding of community bookshops, theatre companies, reading rooms, etc., is at least as important as job creation measures. However, those projects do not fall within the category of preferences specified to date by any of the donor countries.

The USA has been by far the largest contributor to the International Fund. To date a sum of $120 million has been provided and there are firm proposals for further aid in 1989. In June 1988 the United States Congress Committee on Appropriations, in its report to the Senate, commended "the work of the International Fund for Ireland for its work to promote economic development and social reconciliation in Ireland" (at p. 140). However, the Committee went on to state its belief that "what will contribute most effectively to reconciliation and social development is the creation of permanent, long-term jobs in the areas that have suffered most severely from the consequences of the instability of recent years" (at p. 141). This, it said, would remain the primary focus of United States contributions to the Fund. In view of the emphasis which is placed upon social projects by Article 10(a) of the Anglo-Irish Agreement and Article 3 of the Agreement to establish the Fund, and the Board's concern to limit its contributions to the area of job creation, it would appear that the chief donor to the Fund has had considerable influence over the Board in the framing of its main policy.

As the Fund continues to accept applications for financial support, the Board's task is not made easier by uncertainty as to its future life-span and funding prospects. Although there are currently enough resources to justify the Fund's existence for a further two to three years, its progress after that will ultimately depend upon the willingness of national governments or the European Community to support the programmes devised by the Board. And as this is inextricably linked with the state of Anglo-Irish relations, and that of the Agreement in particular, the Fund's future is far from certain.

CHAPTER 4

EXTRADITION

A number of overlapping stages may be delineated in the Irish approach to the extradition of fugitive republican suspects:

1970–1976   Extradition was refused on the basis of the political offence exception and there was no legislation in existence providing for the trial of the relevant offences if committed outside the jurisdiction.

1976–1982   Legislation creating an extra-territorial jurisdiction was enacted and implemented, but extradition was refused.

1982–1987   Judicial re-interpretation of the exception resulted in the granting of extradition.

1987 to date   Legislative changes severely limited the scope of the political offence exception, and certain safeguards were introduced in the extradition process.

1970–1976: strict application of political offence exception

Extradition generally takes place within a framework of bi-lateral or multi-lateral treaties, within which diplomatic channels are used for the presentation of the requisition and supporting documents. Between Ireland and the United Kingdom, however, extradition has, for historical reasons, taken place under a system of reciprocal legislation by which each state backs the other's arrest warrants. In Ireland this arrangement has been based principally on Part III of the Extradition Act 1965 (see below for recent amending legislation) and in the United Kingdom on the Backing of Warrants (Republic of Ireland) Act 1965. In neither case is there a requirement that a prima facie case be established in the courts prior to extradition. In practice once an appropriate warrant was received, it would be endorsed by a Commissioner or Deputy or Assistant Commissioner of the Garda Síochána. It would then be executed and an application made to the District Court for an order for the removal of the suspect (or convicted person) to Britain or Northern Ireland.

In both states what is known in international law as the "political offence exception" applies to the backing of warrants as to other forms of extradition. Under the Irish statute this may be applied under two separate sections. Under section 44 it is provided that a warrant shall not be endorsed for execution if the Minister or the High Court (if the Minister refers the matter to it) so directs; under section 50 it is provided that a person arrested for possible extradition shall be released if the High Court or the Minister so directs. The grounds for making a direction are almost identical under the two sections. Under section 50(2) they are specified as follows:

A direction under this section may be given by the High Court where the Court is of opinion that—
(a) the offence to which the warrant relates is—
(i) a political offence or an offence connected with a political offence, or
(ii) an offence under military law which is not an offence under ordinary criminal law, or
(iii) a revenue offence, or
(b) there are substantial reasons for believing that the person named or described in the warrant will, if removed from the State under this Part, be prosecuted or detained for a political offence or an offence connected with a political offence or an

> offence under military law which is not an offence under ordinary criminal law, or
>
> (c) the offence specified in the warrant does not correspond with any offence under the law of the State which is an indictable offence or is punishable on summary conviction by imprisonment for a maximum period of at least six months.

In practice all cases have been dealt with by applications to the High Court under section 50.

The corresponding provisions of the British statute under section 2(2) are as follows:

> An order [for delivery] shall not be made under subsection (1) of this section if it appears to the court that the offence specified in the warrant does not correspond with any offence under the law of the part of the United Kingdom in which the court acts which is an indictable offence or is punishable on summary conviction with imprisonment for six months; nor shall such an order be made if it is shown to the satisfaction of the court—
>
> (a) that the offence specified in the warrant is an offence of a political character, or an offence under military law which is not also an offence under the general criminal law, or an offence under an enactment relating to taxes, duties or exchange control; or
>
> (b) that there are substantial grounds for believing that the person named or described in the warrant will, if taken to the Republic, be prosecuted or detained for another offence, being an offence of a political character or an offence under military law which is not also an offence under the general criminal law.

There is thus a significant difference in the formulation of the "political offence exception" in the two statutes. The wording "offence of a political character" has been restrictively interpreted by the British and Northern Ireland courts: see, for example, *Re Taylor* [1973] N.I. 159, and *R. v. Governor of Winson Green Prison, ex p. Littlejohn* [1975] 3 All E.R. 208. The Irish Supreme Court in *State (Magee)* v. *O'Rourke* [1971] I.R. 205 was prepared to give a wide interpretation to the corresponding Irish provisions, and held that an IRA raid in 1963 on a British Army barracks in Northern Ireland could be considered a political offence or an offence connected with a political offence. This was followed in a series of unreported High Court decisions in Ireland in the early 1970s in which those whose extradition to Britain or Northern Ireland was sought for offences arising out of the current "Troubles" avoided extradition by successfully pleading the exception.

1976–1982: the Sunningdale compromise on extra-territorial jurisdiction

British Government and unionist dissatisfaction with the attitude of the Irish courts to this issue was frequently voiced, and following the Sunningdale Conference in 1973 a joint Anglo-Irish Law Enforcement Commission was established which re-examined the question of fugitive offenders (*Report of the Law Enforcement Commission* Cmnd. 5627; Prl. 3832). The Commission considered four possible means of dealing with the problem:

> (a) a common law enforcement area in which jurisdiction is exercised by an all-Ireland Court—the all-Ireland court method;
>
> (b) the extradition method;
>
> (c) the conferring of additional extra-territorial jurisdiction upon the courts of each jurisdiction—the extra-territorial method; and
>
> (d) the exercise in each jurisdiction of extra-territorial jurisdiction by special courts consisting of three judges, at least one of whom will be a judge of the other jurisdiction—the mixed courts method.

There was general agreement that the all-Ireland court method was impracticable as an immediate solution and that the mixed courts method offered no legal or procedural advantages over the extra-territorial method. The Irish commissioners rejected the extradition method on the grounds that the non-extradition of political offenders amounted to a rule of international law, and was therefore binding on the state under the terms of Article 29 of the Irish Constitution. Agreement was achieved on the extra-territorial method and this limited consensus was expressed in the Report as follows:

> We are agreed that there are no legal objections to the validity of the extra-territorial method exercised by domestic courts and supplemented by the procedure for taking evidence on commission, described in paragraph 22(b). The members who are against the adoption of extradition recommend the extra-territorial method. The members who favour extradition as their first choice would also recommend the extra-territorial method if extradition is not available. But we all recognise and emphasise that its efficacy depends upon the success of measures designed to bring before the court the relevant evidence, by encouraging witnesses, for both the prosecution and the defence, to cross the border to the place of trial or, where this is not practicable, by securing their attendance to give evidence on commission (paragraph 112(c)).

The recommendations of the Commission were implemented in Ireland in the Criminal Law (Jurisdiction) Act 1976 and in the United Kingdom in the Criminal Jurisdiction Act 1975. Both Acts provide for the exercise of limited extra-territorial jurisdiction in respect of a schedule of terrorist-type offences. The constitutionality of the Irish measure was upheld in *Re Article 26 and the Criminal Law (Jurisdiction) Bill 1975* [1977] I.R. 129. A total of 13 persons have since been tried for extra-territorial offences under the provisions of the Irish legislation of whom 10 were convicted and three acquitted. At the time of writing a further case is being brought under the Act.

1982–1987: judicial re-interpretation of the political offence exception in Ireland

Implementation of the extra-territoriality legislation did not result in the abandoning of attempts to obtain the extradition of IRA and INLA suspects, and since 1982 the Irish Supreme Court has been engaged in a re-interpretation of section 50 of the Extradition Act 1965.

In *McGlinchey* v. *Wren* [1982] I.R. 154 the then Chief Justice, O'Higgins C.J., rejected the plaintiff's claim that the charges which he might face if extradited (other than those for which his extradition was sought) amounted to political offences, and suggested that the test for the application of the exception was whether the "particular circumstances showed that the person charged was at the relevant time engaged, either directly or indirectly, in what reasonable, civilised people would regard as political activity" (*ibid.*, at p. 160). In *Shannon* v. *Fanning* [1984] I.R. 569 the plaintiff's claim that the offences for which his extradition was sought (the murder of the ex-Speaker of the Northern Ireland House of Commons and his son who was a member of the RUC Reserve) were political was also rejected, though members of the Supreme Court differed in the test to be applied. In the view of Chief Justice O'Higgins "the circumstances . . . of the murders in question here were so brutal, cowardly and callous that it would be a distortion of language if they were to be accorded the status of political offences or offences connected with political offences" (*ibid.*, at p. 588).

The decision in *Quinn* v. *Wren* [1985] I.R. 322 marked a further departure. The plaintiff claimed the benefit of the exception by asserting that the offences for which his extradition was sought (fraud) had been carried out for the purposes of the INLA, an organisation whose aims and objectives he described as "the establishment of a thirty-two county workers' republic by force of arms . . . " (*ibid.*, at p. 328). The new Chief Justice, Finlay C.J., rejected the claim because in his view, the achievement of these aims and objectives:

> . . . necessarily and inevitably involves the destruction and setting aside of the Constitution by means expressly or impliedly prohibited by it . . . To interpret the words 'political offence' contained in s.50 of the Act of 1965 so as to grant immunity or protection to a person charged with an offence directly intended to further that objective would be to give to the section a patently unconstitutional construction (*ibid.*, at p. 337).

This line of reasoning, which is clearly distinct from that adopted in *McGlinchey* and *Shannon*, was extended, in a split decision, to IRA cases in *Russell* v. *Fanning* [1988] I.L.R.M. 333. In giving the leading judgment, the Chief Justice (with whom Griffin and Henchy JJ. concurred) stated in relation to the IRA:

> For a person or group of persons, however, to take over or seek to take over the carrying out of a policy of reintegration decided upon by himself or themselves without the authority of the organs of State established by the Constitution is to subvert the Constitution and to usurp the function of Government. In my view, political offence within the meaning of section 50 of the Extradition Act 1965 cannot be construed so as to grant immunity to a person who admittedly has, in respect of the matter with which he is charged, that objective (*ibid.*, at p. 339).

The dissenters were Hederman and McCarthy JJ., both of whom distinguished the case from *Quinn*, and both of whom considered Russell's initial offence to have been a political offence, and his subsequent escape to have involved offences connected with a political offence.

In these cases the Irish judiciary has radically altered its approach to the political offence exception. In the past, a claim that the offence for which extradition was sought was part of a republican paramilitary campaign was sufficient to bring the crime within the scope of the exception. But under *Quinn* and *Russell* an offence committed for the purposes of the IRA or the INLA would automatically be excluded. The way was thus cleared for the extradition of republican suspects even before the ratification by Ireland in 1987 of the European Convention on the Suppression of Terrorism, as promised in the communique of the Hillsborough summit meeting on November 15, 1985. Further clarification will nonetheless be required in order to test the limits of the decisions in *Quinn* and *Russell* since it might be suggested that the effect of these judgments is to deny legal and constitutional rights to those whose activities are deemed to amount to a subversion of the Constitution.

Apart from the changing attitude towards the application of the political offence exception, another noticeable feature of extradition cases in recent years has been the number of extradition applications rejected and orders for removal struck down on "technical" grounds, as shown in Table 1:

Table 1. Extradition to the UK under the Extradition Act 1965 (as originally enacted) for IRA or INLA related offences since December 1982 (as at 12/1/89)*

Extradited	5
Extradition rejected on "technical" grounds	5**
Political offence exception applied	1
Appeals by suspect pending	3
Suspect broke bail while appeal pending	1
Total	15

* Apart from one case (*Maguire*) in which the suspect made a very doubtful claim of political motivation.
** Appeal apparently pending in one case.

In addition a number of those eventually extradited have been acquitted. In practice, extradition has thus proved less effective than some had predicted, as shown in Table 2:

Table 2. Outcome of extraditions (under Table 1) to the UK (as at 12/1/89)

Convicted and acquitted on appeal	1
Convicted and convictions upheld	0
Acquitted at first instance	1
Case struck out	1
Proceedings pending or in progress	2
Total	5

1987 to date: The European Convention on the Suppression of Terrorism and the Irish legislation of 1987

The changing attitude of the courts to the interpretation of the political offence exception made it easier for the Irish Government to give its pledge in the communique issued on the signing of the Anglo-Irish Agreement that it would accede to the 1977 European Convention on the Suppression of Terrorism.

Article 1 of the Convention sets out a list of offences which are not to be considered political for the purposes of extradition between contracting states and Article 2 permits states to regard other serious offences against persons and property as not political:

Article 1

For the purposes of extradition between Contracting States, none of the following offences shall be regarded as a political offence or as an offence connected with a political offence or as an offence inspired by political motives:

(a) an offence within the scope of the Convention for the Suppression of Unlawful Seizure of Aircraft, signed at The Hague on 16 December 1970;

(b) an offence within the scope of the Convention for the Suppression of Unlawful Acts against the Safety of Civil Aviation, signed at Montreal on 23 September 1971;

(c) a serious offence involving an attack against the life, physical integrity or liberty of internationally protected persons, including diplomatic agents;

(d) an offence involving kidnapping, the taking of a hostage or serious unlawful detention;

(e) an offence involving the use of a bomb, grenade, rocket, automatic firearm or letter or parcel bomb if this use endangers persons;

(*f*) an attempt to commit any of the foregoing offences or participation as an accomplice of a person who commits or attempts
to commit such an offence.

Article 2

(1) For the purposes of extradition between Contracting States, a
Contracting State may decide not to regard as a political offence or as
an offence connected with a political offence or as an offence inspired
by political motives a serious offence involving an act of violence,
other than one covered by Article 1, against the life, physical integrity
or liberty of a person.
(2) The same shall apply to a serious offence involving an act against
property, other than one covered by Article 1, if the act created a collective danger for persons.
(3) The same shall apply to an attempt to commit any of the foregoing
offences or participation as an accomplice of a person who commits or
attempts to commit such an offence.

Under Article 13, however, states may enter a reservation preserving the
right to regard Article 1 offences as political:

(1) Any State may, at the time of signature or when depositing its
instrument of ratification, acceptance or approval, declare that it
reserves the right to refuse extradition in respect of any offence men-
tioned in Article 1 which it considers to be a political offence, an
offence connected with a political offence or an offence inspired by
political motives, provided that it undertakes to take into due consideration, when evaluating the character of the offence, any particularly serious aspects of the offence, including:
  (*a*) that it created a collective danger to the life, physical integrity
       or liberty of persons; or
  (*b*) that it affected persons foreign to the motives behind it; or
  (*c*) that cruel or vicious means have been used in the commission
       of the offence.

It is thus permissible for a state to ratify the Convention and yet, by
entering an Article 13 reservation, to refuse extradition for many offences
connected with the Northern Ireland conflict. In such circumstances the
refusing state would be obliged under Article 7 to submit the case to its
competent authorities for the purposes of prosecution. A substantial
number of states, notably France, Belgium and the Netherlands, entered
reservations of this kind in signing the Convention. This was not the course
taken by Ireland, which in the Extradition (European Convention on the
Suppression of Terrorism) Act 1987 provided for the ratification of the
Convention (including a partial adoption of Article 2) without any article
of reservation. The legislation was enacted in January and was to come into
force on December 1, 1987. The purpose of the delay was to allow further
discussion with the British Government on possible changes in the Diplock
Court system and when the Irish suggestions were rejected there was some
speculation that the implementation of the Convention might be further
delayed. However, the Enniskillen bombing, the O'Grady kidnapping and
mutilation, and the *Eksund* arms cargo all created an atmosphere in which
non-implementation was politically impossible. Nonetheless, the fact that
previous extraditions had eventually resulted in the release of the accused,
together with continuing reservations about the Diplock Court system, and
concern about the cases of the Birmingham Six, the Guildford Four and
the Maguires led to sustained pressure for the introduction of new safeguards in the extradition process. The Irish Government eventually
secured the implementation of the Convention on December 1, 1987 but

on December 14 new safeguards were introduced in the Extradition (Amendment) Act 1987.

The Extradition (Amendment) Act is not "free standing" but operates in conjunction with Part III of the Extradition Act 1965. It permits the refusal of extradition when by reason of lapse of time or other exceptional circumstances it would be unjust, oppressive or invidious to extradite (s.50(2)(b) of the 1965 Act as inserted by s.2(1)(b) of the Extradition (Amendment) Act 1987). Provision is made for the introduction at a future date of both a speciality requirement and a bar on re-extradition to third countries. But the central feature of this measure is the new scrutinizing role given to the Irish Attorney-General in dealing with British extradition warrants. Under section 44B of the Extradition Act 1965 as inserted by section 2(1) of the Extradition (Amendment) Act 1987 the Irish Attorney-General is to give a direction that a warrant not be endorsed (and therefore that extradition to the United Kingdom not proceed) unless—

> . . . having considered such information as he deems appropriate, [he] is of opinion that—
> (a) there is a clear intention to prosecute or, as the case may be, to continue the prosecution of, the person named or described in the warrant concerned for the offence specified therein in a place in relation to which this Part [III] applies,
> and
> (b) such intention is founded on the existence of sufficient evidence.

These provisions have proved controversial. Concern has been voiced that they may be in conflict with Article 34.1 of the Irish Constitution, as it could be argued that the exercise by the Irish Attorney-General of his duties under the Act amounts to the administration of justice, a function which, under that Article, is reserved for judges appointed in the manner provided by the Constitution. Article 37, however, permits the exercise of "limited" judicial functions in matters other than criminal matters, to be conferred by law on persons who are not judges. Unlike the course taken in relation to the Criminal Law (Jurisdiction) Bill 1975, the Extradition (Amendment) Bill 1987 was not referred by the President (who acts in such cases after consultation with the Council of State) to the Supreme Court for a ruling on its constitutionality. The issue is therefore certain to be raised in the courts. This challenge will have the effect of preventing any extradition under the terms of the Act pending the outcome of the proceedings. Another problematic area is whether the decision of the Attorney-General is subject to judicial review. Yet another is the question of what supporting documentation is required of the British side in order to satisfy the requirements of the Act that the Irish Attorney-General consider "such information as he deems appropriate." This issue was the cause of the dispute between the British and Irish Attorneys-General which followed the implementation of the Act. In May 1988, despite the failure to agree on any standard procedure, it was agreed that the required documentation would be decided on a case-by-case basis, and it appears to have been on this footing that cases since then have been processed.

The Act was to expire 12 months after the date of its passage unless a resolution was passed by each House of the Oireachtas before then declaring that it should continue in operation thereafter. The required Dáil resolution was made on December 6, 1988. Thus the legislation can now continue in force indefinitely, though a review of extradition arrangements has been promised. During the debate on the resolution, the Taoiseach informed the Dáil that since the previous year, 17 warrants had been received under the Act in relation to all types of offence. Of these, four were recalled before it was established whether the Act was complied with;

in seven cases the warrants fell outside the scope of the Act because they related to someone already convicted; in four cases, the warrants were cleared for endorsement, and papers were still being considered in regard to two cases.

Further issues have been raised in the case of Father Patrick Ryan. Following the refusal of extradition by the Belgian authorities and the return of Ryan to Ireland, extradition was refused by the Irish Attorney-General in December 1988. Though it was accepted that extradition could have been granted under the terms of the 1987 legislation in respect of two of the warrants under which Ryan was sought, the Attorney-General decided not to authorise it on the ground that comments on the case in the British press and in Parliament at Westminster made it unlikely that Ryan could expect a fair trial in a British court. In a statement explaining his action he asserted that, independently of the provisions of the Extradition (Amendment) Act 1987, the Attorney-General must ensure that a proposed extradition application to the courts complies with all other requirements of the law and Constitution of the state, and that every citizen had a constitutional right to a fair trial. He indicated that the use of the procedure for extra-territorial jurisdiction would be more appropriate in the Ryan case, and at the time of writing this possibility seems likely to be accepted by the British authorities.

The current state of extradition applications in relation to paramilitary suspects under the legislation as amended in 1987 is shown in Table 3.

Table 3. Extradition to the U.K. for IRA or INLA related offences under the procedures as amended by the Extradition (Amendment) Act 1987 (as at 12/1/89)

Extradited	0
Extradition ordered by District Court	1*
Extradition rejected on "technical" grounds	1*
Extradition refused by Attorney-General on "fair trial" grounds	1
	—
Total	3

* Appeal pending.

CHAPTER 5

REACTIONS AND ACHIEVEMENTS

Political reaction

The signing of the Anglo-Irish Agreement was received with general acclaim in Britain, Ireland and the rest of the world. The major exceptions, as might have been anticipated, were unionists in Northern Ireland and republicans in both parts of Ireland.

(i) *Reaction in Britain*

The general all-party support for the Agreement in Britain was expressed by the overwhelming vote in the House of Commons on November 27, 1985 (473 votes to 47) and in speeches by the main party leaders. Mrs Thatcher emphasised the goal of reconciling the two communities in Northern Ireland:

> The Unionist community . . . have a right to feel secure about Northern Ireland's position as part of the United Kingdom. This Agreement by reinforcing the principle of consent should make them feel more secure, not only today but in the future. Unionists have the assurance that neither an Irish Government nor of course a British Government will try to impose new constitutional arrangements upon them against their will. The nationalist community think of themselves as Irish in terms of their identity, their social and cultural traditions and their political aspirations. The House can respect their identity too and acknowledge their aspirations even though we may not see the prospect of their fulfilment. The only lasting way to put an end to the violence and achieve the peace and stability in Northern Ireland is reconciliations between these two communities. That is the goal of this Agreement (H.C. Deb. cols. 747–748 (November 27, 1985)).

The leader of the Labour Party, Mr. Kinnock, likewise made a commitment of support for the Agreement notwithstanding his party's preference for Irish unity by consent:

> As a matter of policy and of commitment the Labour Party wants to see Ireland united by consent, and we are committed to working actively to secure that consent. However, that is not the reason for our action in approving the Hillsborough accord. We recognise that the priority is reconciliation in the communities of Northern Ireland and between the communities of Northern Ireland. It is that objective which brings our consent (*ibid.*, col. 758).

The only dissent from this general consensus in support of the Agreement was by Unionist MPs and a small group of Tory MPs who supported them. A Government minister, Ian Gow, resigned on the issue.

(ii) *Reaction in Ireland*

In Ireland the formal reaction to the Agreement among politicians followed traditional party lines. The Government secured a small but satisfactory majority by 88 votes to 75 in Dáil Éireann on November 21, 1985, and a significantly larger majority in Seanad Éireann by 37 votes to 16 on November 28, 1985. The significance of the Agreement was marked by the four days of debate accorded to it by Dáil Éireann. But the approach of the main party leaders differed on its constitutional implications. The Taoiseach, Dr. Fitzgerald, argued that the Agreement advanced the nationalist aspiration to Irish unity:

It was the clear view of our Government from the outset that in the situation now existing in Northern Ireland it would be impossible to end the alienation of the minority from the structures of government and from the security and judicial systems unless there existed within the structures of the government of Northern Ireland a significant role for the Irish Government, towards which the Nationalist minority in Northern Ireland look—just as the Unionist majority look to the Government of the United Kingdom. . . .

But while . . . the Agreement diminishes in no way the Nationalist aspiration to unity, and of its very nature cannot affect our constitutional position, the third clause of article 1 of the Agreement advances that aspiration significantly. For in that clause the British Government as well as the Irish Government declare that, if in the future a majority of the people of Northern Ireland clearly wish for and formally consent to the establishment of a united Ireland, they will introduce and support in their respective Parliaments legislation to give effect to that wish.

The commitment in this clause to introduce such legislation is the first clear affirmation in any binding Anglo-Irish agreement since 1921 that Britain has no interest in the continuing division of this island and that its presence in this island, undertaking the responsibility of government in Northern Ireland, continues solely because this is the wish of a majority of the people of that area and will not continue beyond the point when that consent is changed into consent to Irish unity (*Dáil Debates* cols. 2562 and 2570 (November 19, 1985)).

But the leader of Fianna Fáil, Mr. Haughey, argued that the Irish Government by signing the Agreement had abandoned Ireland's constitutional claim to the unity of its national territory:

We are deeply concerned that by signing this Agreement the Irish Government are acting in a manner repugnant to the Constitution of Ireland by fully accepting British sovereignty over a part of the national territory and by purporting to give legitimacy to a British administration in Ireland. By confirming what is called the constitutional status of Northern Ireland as an integral part of the United Kingdom in this Agreement we will do serious damage in the eyes of the world to Ireland's historic and legitimate claim to the unity of her territory. It is also our view that the Agreement will lead the Irish Government into an impossible political situation, in which they will find themselves assuming responsibility for actions and becoming involved in situations, particularly in the security field, over which they will have no control (*ibid.*, col. 2581).

In support of this position he moved a detailed amendment to the motion before the Dáil setting out his party's traditional position:

having regard to Articles 2 and 3 of the Constitution of Ireland;
recalling the unanimous Declaration of Dáil Éireann adopted on the joint proposition of An Taoiseach, John A. Costello, and the Leader of the Opposition, Eamon de Valera, on 10 May 1949 solemnly reasserting the indefeasible right of the Irish Nation to the unity and integrity of the national territory;
recalling that all the parties in the New Ireland Forum were convinced that a united Ireland in the form of a sovereign independent state would offer the best and more durable basis for peace and stability;
reaffirming the unanimous conclusion of the Report of the New Ireland Forum that the particular structure of political unity which the Forum would wish to see established is a unitary state achieved by agreement and consent, embracing the whole island of Ireland and

providing irrevocable guarantees for the protection and preservation of both the unionist and nationalist identities;

while recognising the urgent need that exists for substantial improvement in the situation and circumstances of the nationalist section of the community in the North of Ireland and approving any effective measures which may be undertaken for that purpose, refuses to accept any recognition of British sovereignty over any part of the national territory;

and requests the Government to call upon the British Government to join in convening under the joint auspices of both Governments a constitutional conference representative of all the traditions in Ireland to formulate new constitutional arrangements which would lead to uniting all the people of Ireland in peace and harmony (*ibid.*, cols. 2580–2581).

A few other Deputies and Senators, notably Mary Robinson, expressed concern that the Agreement by effectively excluding unionists from participation in the new arrangements could not assist in achieving lasting peace and stability.

It should be noted that following the clear evidence in successive opinion polls (see below) of general support for the Agreement by the Irish electorate the opposition to it by members of Fianna Fáil became more muted. In the run-up to the Irish General Election of February 1988 Mr. Haughey made it clear that if elected he would regard a Fianna Fáil Government as bound by the Agreement and that it would continue to participate in the Anglo-Irish Intergovernmental Conference.

(iii) *Reaction in Northern Ireland*

In Northern Ireland open support for the Agreement was limited to members and supporters of the Social Democratic and Labour Party, whose leader, John Hume, had played a leading role in the New Ireland Forum and who had been kept informed of progress in the negotiations leading to the signing of the Agreement. In the debate on the Agreement at Westminster Mr. Hume emphasised the role of the Agreement in recognising the validity of both traditions in Northern Ireland:

The people of Ireland are divided on sovereignty. They will be united only by a process of reconciliation in which both traditions in Ireland can take part and agree. If that happens, it will lead to the only unity that matters—a unity that accepts that the essence of unity is the acceptance of diversity. . . . For the first time [the Agreement] sets up a framework that addresses the problem of the interlocking relationships between the people of both Irelands. It is the approach of maximum consensus. It is the way of minimum risk. For the first time . . . it respects the equal validity of both traditions. . . . It is not a concession to me or to the people whom I represent. It is an absolute right to the legitimate expression of our identity and of the people I represent. . . .
The recognition of the equal validity of both traditions removes for the first time every excuse for the use of violence by anybody in Ireland to achieve his objective (H.C. Deb. col. 783 (November 26, 1985)).

In subsequent speeches he laid equal emphasis on the commitment by Britain to accept the unification of Ireland if the people of Northern Ireland consent (speech to SDLP Party Conference, November 21–23, 1986).

The reaction of unionists was almost universally hostile and was expressed with a vehemence which must have surprised those who had sought in the Agreement to recognise and protect the interests of unionists as well as nationalists. At a rally at the City Hall in Belfast on November 23, 1985, attended by an estimated 100,000 to 200,000 people, the Democratic Unionist Party Leader, Dr. Ian Paisley, stated that unionists would "never, never, never" accept the Agreement. In the Westminster debate the Official Unionist Party Leader, James Molyneaux, stressed that it could not bring either peace, stability or reconciliation (H.C. Deb. col. 763 (November 26, 1985)). Following this debate the Official and Democratic Unionist MPs withdrew from the House of Commons and resigned their seats to ensure a kind of referendum on the Agreement. At the subsequent bye-elections held on January 23, 1986 anti-Agreement candidates polled 418,230 votes, representing about 40 per cent. of the total electorate, though one seat in Newry and Armagh was lost to the SDLP. The main Unionist parties also established a Grand Committee of the Northern Ireland Assembly to consider their response. The First Report of the Committee, published on January 29, 1986, reached the following conclusions (Northern Ireland Assembly 237–I, pp. 72–73):

. . .

(3) The manner in which the Agreement was negotiated clearly indicates that it is designed to operate to the detriment of the majority of the people of Northern Ireland; that there is no equality of treatment in the approach to the negotiations and there has been no willingness on the part of Her Majesty's Government to enter into serious discussions with the representatives of the majority of the people.

(4) The Agreement does not give any added recognition to the status of Northern Ireland; rather than accept the right of the people of Northern Ireland to determine their future, the Agreement attempts to subvert that right.

(5) The Intergovernmental Conference is a joint authority in embryo, which if allowed to develop will become the effective government of Northern Ireland within its field of activity.

. . .

(7) The Agreement clearly diminishes British sovereignty in Northern Ireland by admitting a foreign Government into the structure and processes of government of Northern Ireland: Northern Ireland is no longer a part of the United Kingdom on the same basis as Great Britain and the people of Northern Ireland are denied equality of treatment, status and esteem with their fellow citizens.

. . .

(9) The changes in security and other policies adumbrated in the Agreement will only lead to greater insecurity and instability and that this Agreement will not lead to peace and reconciliation.

(10) There is no prospect of devolution while the Agreement remains; that devolution is now in the effective gift of the SDLP and is unlikely to be offered on terms acceptable to unionists; that devolution will not eliminate the Inter-governmental Conference; that the requirements for devolution are unjust in that greater acceptance is required to diminish the Agreement than was needed to establish it.

(11) In total the Agreement is discriminatory; it does not provide for equality of treatment either within Northern Ireland or within the United Kingdom; that it is irreformable—that there are no changes which can make this framework acceptable and it must be removed.

Following this Report the Unionist parties refused to carry out the statutory functions of the Assembly which was eventually wound up by the Secretary of State in June 1986.

The response of Provisional Sinn Féin was equally dismissive of the Agreement, though for diametrically opposed reasons. In a considered speech on May 4, 1986 Danny Morrison concluded that the Agreement, "in return for accepting British sovereignty in the six counties and the loyalist veto" granted Dublin only a consultative role in Northern affairs, far short of the least demand of the three Forum options and that a primary objective was "stabilising the six-county state." Sinn Féin has continued to demand a total British withdrawal and to express support for "armed struggle" as a legitimate means to achieve it.

The smaller Northern Ireland parties have adopted less clear-cut positions. The Alliance Party, "although critical of the fact that the Agreement was conceived in secrecy and without prior consultation with the Northern Ireland constitutional parties . . . resolved to give it a fair chance to achieve its objectives of peace, reconciliation and political stability" (*Manifesto* 1987). The Workers Party gave its reluctant support to the Agreement on the ground that while its objectives were sound the strategy of excluding the Unionists was undemocratic. It later argued for a suspension of the Agreement to enable all-party talks in Northern Ireland to take place (*The Socialist Perspective on Northern Ireland and the Anglo-Irish Agreement*, November 1986).

(iv) *Talks about Talks*

Throughout the first three years of the operation of the Agreement there have been sustained attempts to involve the main Unionist Party leaders, Mr. Molyneaux and Dr. Paisley, in discussions with the British Government on how the objective of restoring devolved government in Northern Ireland might be achieved within the framework of the Agreement or parallel to it. The initial round of discussions in 1986 were broken off when it became clear that the British Government was not prepared to do more than "operate the Agreement sensitively" while the Unionist leaders insisted on at least a suspension of its operation. There was also dissension among Unionists over methods of opposing the Agreement. A one-day strike on March 3, 1986 was organised by the newly formed Ulster Clubs and others opposed to any form of negotiation. But both the Official Unionists and the Democratic Unionists eventually agreed on a policy of non-co-operation with the processes of government, notably by suspending or adjourning district council meetings so as to prevent any business being transacted. A working party was set up to report on possible strategies. Its report, *An end to Drift*, was partially published in July 1987 and recommended renewed discussions on an alternative to the Agreement though the option of pursuing independence for Northern Ireland in the event of failure was expressly reserved.

In the latter part of 1987, following preparatory discussions by leading churchmen and others, direct talks between the two Unionist leaders and the Northern Ireland Office were resumed to see if a formula could be found which would allow substantive talks to begin. These "talks about talks" gradually merged into general discussions and a working document was delivered by the Unionist leaders to the Secretary of State for Northern Ireland in 1988. Since then little formal progress has been made. The British Government has refused to agree to the Unionist pre-conditions of a suspension of the Agreement and the closure of the Secretariat at Maryfield and no further serious negotiations have taken place in the run-up to the formal review of the Agreement under Article 11 (see above). Informal discussions on the conditions under which more formal talks might begin, however, have been continued, notably at and following a meeting at Duisburg in West Germany in October 1988.

There have been similar difficulties in respect of direct talks between the Unionist parties and the SDLP. Though the SDLP has repeatedly expressed its willingness to enter into talks without pre-conditions, it has in practice made its commitment to the continued operation of the Agreement clear. Its separate discussions with Sinn Féin during 1988 over the legitimacy and effects of the continued armed struggle also made it politically impractical for direct talks with the Unionists to be initiated at that time.

Opinion polls

The attitude of members of the public to the Agreement has been periodically tested in both parts of Ireland. The results show considerable variation in responses to particular questions or aspects of the Agreement but general consistency among the main groups polled, unionists and nationalists in Northern Ireland, and the electorate in the rest of Ireland.

(i) *Polls in Northern Ireland*

A poll carried out by MORI for the *Sunday Times* immediately after the signing of the Agreement suggested that 75 per cent. of Protestants would vote against the Agreement in a referendum while 65 per cent. of Catholics would vote for it (*Sunday Times*, November 24, 1985). Remarkably similar figures were produced in an Ulster Marketing Surveys poll for the BBC early in 1986: 76 per cent. of Protestants said they were opposed to the Agreement and only 8 per cent. supported it; while 54 per cent. of Catholics supported it and only 10 per cent. were opposed to it (see *Fortnight*, February 10, 1986). But a poll by Coopers & Lybrand for the *Belfast Telegraph* in January 1986 indicated that these responses were linked to very different perceptions of what the Agreement meant: most Protestants (53%) thought it gave the Irish Government a voice in decision-making on Northern Ireland which was unacceptable to almost all Protestants (87%); most Catholics (51%) thought it gave only a consultative role, though a role in decision-making would have been acceptable to more (60%) (*Belfast Telegraph*, January 15, 1986).

More recent polls have not asked the same questions, but indicate increasing disenchantment with the Agreement in both communities. A poll carried out by Coopers & Lybrand for *Fortnight* in February 1988 indicated that 81 per cent. of Catholics and 72 per cent. of Protestants felt that the Agreement had not benefited the nationalist community; 94 per cent. of Protestants and 88 per cent. of Catholics felt that it had not benefited the unionist community (*Fortnight*, April 7, 1988). Another poll by Coopers & Lybrand for the *Belfast Telegraph* in September 1988 indicated that 62 per cent. of Protestants were just as opposed to the Agreement as they had been initially and that only 5 per cent. were less opposed and only 5 per cent. just as much in favour; among Catholics 34 per cent. were just as much in favour and 26 per cent. less in favour, while 15 per cent. were just as opposed (*Belfast Telegraph*, October 4, 1988).

(ii) *Polls in Ireland*

Initial polls of the Irish electorate indicated substantial and increasing support for the Agreement: an MRBI poll for the *Irish Times* in November 1985 indicated that 59 per cent. approved of the Agreement while 29 per cent. disapproved; by February 1986 69 per cent. approved and only 20 per cent. disapproved (*Irish Times*, February 12, 1986). Since then it would appear that no opinion polls have been conducted in Ireland specifically on the Agreement.

Achievements

Public attitudes to the Agreement were initially related to perceptions of what was intended and what might be achieved under it. More recently they have been related to perceptions of what has been achieved in the initial years, though people in Britain and Ireland and members of the two communities in Northern Ireland clearly have different perceptions of the primary objectives of the Agreement. People in Britain probably focus their attention on the general objective of achieving peace, stability and reconciliation in Northern Ireland; those in Ireland probably focus their attention on improvements in the situation of nationalists, both economically and politically, as well as on those more general objectives; unionists in Northern Ireland probably focus most attention on levels of terrorist activity and other security matters; nationalists in Northern Ireland probably focus most attention on their own economic and political situation.

A further difficulty in assessing achievements during the first three years of the Agreement arises from the tacit agreement by both the British and Irish Governments not to emphasise the contribution of the Anglo-Irish Conference to specific decisions and a corresponding emphasis by the British Government on the separate development of its own policies on relevant matters. This approach was intended to minimise unionist reaction to the establishment and operation of the new arrangements. But it has also resulted in a general perception of inactivity and ineffectiveness on the part of the Conference and its Secretariat which is to some extent misleading. Those who have been directly involved in the operation of the Conference and its Secretariat typically give a very different assessment of its usefulness and achievements from those who have observed its working from the outside.

A balanced assessment of the achievements of the new structure set up under the Agreement must take account of these different views of the primary objectives of the Agreement and of the contribution of the Conference and its Secretariat to decisions on particular matters. There can therefore be no single judgment on the success or failure of the Agreement. The position in respect of each of the main objectives may be summarised under the broad headings of the Agreement itself.

(i) *Peace, stability and reconciliation*

It is clear that this general objective of the Agreement, as set out in the Preamble, has not been achieved, though it was always anticipated that attempts on either side to break the resolve of the two Governments would result in an increase in paramilitary activity. In practice the initial upsurge in paramilitary activity on the loyalist side, notably in respect of intimidation, in the early part of 1986 was not sustained though it contributed to a further and more lasting increase in the residential segregation of the two communities. On the republican side there has been some increase in the general level of paramilitary activity, as was predicted, though the number of members of the security forces on and off duty who have been assassinated remained relatively constant until 1988. The general picture in respect of the various forms of paramilitary and terrorist activity in the years before and after the signing of the Agreement as measured in the official security statistics are set out in the accompanying Table.

Summary of paramilitary and terrorist activity: 1969–88

	1969–70 (average)	1971–76 (average)	1977–80 (average)	1981	1982	1983	1984	1985	1986	1987	1988
Shootings	143	4053	801	1142	547	424	334	237	392	674	537
Explosions	81	870	381	398	219	266	193	148	172	236	253
Deaths:											
RUC/RUCR	1	15	12	21	12	18	9	23	12	16	6
UDR	—	11	10	13	7	10	10	4	8	8	12
Army	—	43	19	10	21	5	9	2	4	3	21
Civilian	17	206	55	57	57	44	36	25	37	66	54
Totals	19*	275	95*	101	97	77	64	54	61	93	93
Injuries	838	2935	1011	1350	525	510	866	916	1450	1130	1047

*The individual figures do not add up to the total due to rounding of the respective averages.

The extent to which these figures and trends can be attributed directly to reaction to the Agreement as opposed to such factors as the receipt by the IRA of massive new supplies of arms and explosives during 1987 is debatable. But it cannot seriously be argued that the Agreement has resulted in any marked improvement in the general security situation or in better intercommunal relations.

(ii) *The Intergovernmental Conference*

At an institutional level the establishment of the Anglo-Irish Intergovernmental Conference and Secretariat must be judged to have been a success. Despite considerable local opposition to the establishment of the Secretariat at Maryfield in Belfast and repeated political strains at the highest level between the British and Irish Governments, the Secretariat has carried out its role of maintaining continuous contact between the two administrations on both contentious and non-contentious issues. Regular ministerial meetings have likewise been continued even when there have been deep and potentially disruptive differences in approach on specific issues such as the decision by the British Government not to institute prosecutions following the Stalker/Sampson inquiry and the repeated disputes over the response of the Irish Government in respect of extradition. If the new institutions have not always resolved conflicts on major policy issues, they have at least resulted in the better management of these conflicts.

(iii) *Political matters*

Achievements in respect of political matters under Articles 4 to 6 of the Agreement have been satisfactory on minor items but less so on more fundamental objectives, as the following summary indicates:

Devolution (Article 4)

There has been no real progress towards this objective: the existence of the Agreement has proved as much of a barrier to unionist co-operation after 1985 as the absence of any Irish dimension before 1985 was to SDLP co-operation. There has been no observable encouragement from the Irish side on this matter.

Recognising and accommodating the rights and identities of the two communities in Northern Ireland (Article 5)

The British Government has taken action on some issues of concern to nationalists, such as the repeal of the Flags and Emblems Display Act (Northern Ireland) 1954 and the disenfranchisement of certain Irish citizens from voting in local and Assembly elections in Northern Ireland. Less has been done to give formal recognition to the Irish language. No attempt has been made to give more general statutory or constitutional recognition to communal rights or identities.

The protection of human rights (Article 5)

The only proposal in this sphere was for a joint declaration by both Governments and has not been pursued. No other action has been taken.

The prevention of discrimination (Article 5)

The British Government has been persuaded to introduce more effective legislation in this field by combined pressure from supporters of the McBride Principles in the USA, the Standing Advisory Commission on Human Rights for Northern Ireland and the Irish Government through the Conference.

Representation for nationalists on official bodies (Article 5)

There has been no outwardly observable change in practice in this sphere, and no compelling case for any such change has been made.

Reciprocal action in Ireland and Britain (Article 5)

No measures of this kind have been discussed or implemented.

(iv) *Legal matters (Article 8)*

There has been little progress on the principal objectives of increasing public confidence among nationalists in the administration of justice; the apparent influence of the Conference on such matters as the abandonment of supergrass trials has been offset by its lack of influence on such matters as prosecutions following the Stalker/Sampson inquiry. No major steps have been taken in respect of the harmonisation of the law or the development of mixed courts. Extradition has continued to prove both ineffective and a major cause of conflict, and the structures for extra-territorial jurisdiction have not been developed.

(v) *Security matters (Articles 7 and 9)*

Security problems have been regularly discussed, though little detailed information has been released. It appears that some progress has been made in improving operational contacts and co-operation between the police forces on either side of the border, though no detailed programme of work for encouraging more general contacts has apparently been developed or implemented. Less progress has been made in securing support for or co-operation with the security forces by nationalists within Northern Ireland. The achievements that have been influenced through the Conference, such as the implementation of a new Police Code and more acceptable ground rules in respect of the routeing of marches, have not been publicly identified with the Conference.

(vi) *Economic co-operation (Article 10)*

There has been little observable change in the level of activity in this sphere, though meetings between officials and, less frequently, between ministers have been continued on a wide range of issues. Though international support for the International Fund for Ireland has been obtained, the initial funding programmes have not been such as to secure much greater public support for or recognition of the contribution of the Agreement.

CHAPTER 6

FUTURE DEVELOPMENTS

It is difficult to make an assessment of the future of the Anglo-Irish Agreement or any recommendations for its amendment without taking a position on the merits of its underlying objectives. Many unionists would like to see the end of the Agreement because they are unwilling to accept any formal recognition of an Irish dimension in the structures and processes of government in Northern Ireland. Many nationalists would also like to see an end to it because they are unwilling to accept any formal recognition of the legitimacy of Northern Ireland as a governmental unit within the United Kingdom whether or not there is any recognition of the Irishness of a substantial number of the people who live in it. Those who give their general support to the Agreement, even if they have reservations on matters of detail, reject both these absolute positions and accept the underlying objective of giving recognition to both the British and Irish traditions within Northern Ireland as an established governmental unit.

The arguments in favour of this approach, which we have set out at length elsewhere (see K. Boyle & T. Hadden, *Ireland: A Positive Proposal* (Penguin Books, 1985)), are that it is more likely to produce long term peace and stability than any other practical option. First, it is clear that the unification of Ireland in any form is totally unacceptable to unionists and that the integration of Northern Ireland with the rest of Britain without any recognition of an Irish dimension is unacceptable to most nationalists. Secondly, it is clear that while repartition of Northern Ireland could be justified on demographic grounds it could not resolve the underlying problem without a very substantial movement of population, notably from West Belfast, which virtually no-one is prepared to contemplate. Thirdly, it is clear that continued government of Northern Ireland on a long term basis by a form of joint authority is likely to prove inherently unstable, in that both sides would naturally seek to put pressure on the British and Irish Governments to seek or concede further constitutional changes; such a regime would also be inherently undemocratic in that politicians within Northern Ireland would have little effective influence on the course of events. The re-establishment of self-government on a power-sharing basis within the existing constitutional structure, as proposed in the Anglo-Irish Agreement, provides the best hope for a stable settlement and has regularly secured the maximum level of support from both communities in the opinion polls. The purpose of this concluding section is not to repeat those arguments in detail, but to make some further positive proposals in the context of the current review of the Agreement under Article 11 with a view to making better progress than has proved possible in the first three years of its operation.

The objectives of the Agreement

For this purpose it is necessary to restate in simple terms the main policy objectives of the Agreement: to pursue political reconciliation within Northern Ireland and between Britain and Ireland as a whole; to guarantee the right of the people of Northern Ireland to choose between continued membership of the United Kingdom and a united Ireland; to guarantee fair treatment and equality of esteem for members of both the unionist and nationalist communities there; to encourage the development of devolved government within Northern Ireland on a basis which is acceptable to both communities, and until that can be achieved to permit the Irish Government to represent the interests of the nationalist community through the Anglo-Irish Intergovernmental Conference; and, finally, to agree on security policies that are consistent with these objectives.

There are a number of reasons for the disappointing progress towards these objectives during the first three years of the Agreement. One of the main problems has been the refusal of almost all unionists to co-operate in any way and their insistence on the abandonment or at least the suspension of the Agreement as a pre-condition to talks on devolution. The British Government has responded to this intransigent attitude by adopting an extremely cautious position over action under other parts of the Agreement for fear of increasing unionist opposition. In particular it has been reluctant to act quickly to improve equality of opportunity and esteem for members of the nationalist community or to introduce the kind of reforms in security policy and in the administration of justice which would increase the confidence of nationalists. For its part the Irish Government, especially after the defeat of Dr. Fitzgerald's Coalition and the advent of Mr. Haughey's new Fianna Fáil Government early in 1987, has focused almost exclusively on nationalist concerns and has failed to take any action to reassure unionists either by emphasising or strengthening the constitutional guarantee under Article 1 or by giving positive support to any form of devolution.

The opponents of the Agreement on either side, both political and paramilitary, have taken advantage of this general lack of momentum and have been able to ensure that the agenda of successive meetings of the Conference has been dominated by matters of public order and security. The Conference has thus been seen largely as a forum for crisis management of the kind so rightly condemned by the New Ireland Forum and has been unable to develop and lead public opinion towards the acceptance and implementation of the objectives of the Agreement. The main achievement of the Conference has in a sense been in not breaking down altogether in the face of successive confrontations on security and related matters, such as the routeing of Orange marches in 1986, the continuing controversy over the Stalker/Sampson inquiry into alleged "shoot-to-kill" incidents and successive disputes over extradition.

Restoring the momentum of the Agreement

If this deadlock is to be broken and the positive momentum of the Agreement restored some action will have to be taken following the current review of the working of the Conference under Article 11. If a "minimalist" approach is adopted this might be limited to a general restatement of the commitment of the two Governments to the terms of the Agreement and the continued operation of the Conference. This is unlikely to prove effective. If public confidence in Britain and Ireland and in Northern Ireland in the value of the Agreement as more than a formal procedure for intergovernmental consultation is to be sustained more cogent evidence of the commitment of the Governments to achieving its stated objectives will be required.

The principal objective must be to secure the consent of the unionist community in Northern Ireland to the broad objectives of the Agreement, since they cannot in practice be achieved without unionist co-operation. This suggests that two levels of action may need to be identified: first, some relatively minor changes in the procedures and possibly the wording of the Agreement to help ensure that its objectives can be more effectively pursued in advance of full unionist participation; and, secondly, some more fundamental amendments to the Agreement designed to accommodate full unionist participation. These will be considered in turn.

It must be stressed in this context that the view which has sometimes been put forward in official and other quarters that the Agreement as an internationally binding treaty is unchangeable and that the current review is formally limited to a consideration of how it can be made to work better is legally inaccurate. As explained in the Introduction above, there is no limit in purely formal terms to the extent of any review of the Agreement. In international law, as codified in the Vienna Convention on the Law of Treaties, the Agreement may be clarified or amended at any time by means of a protocol provided both parties agree. It may also be abandoned and replaced by a new Agreement if both parties agree. And its operation may be suspended at any time if both parties agree. These provisions apply as much to the allegedly entrenched guarantee on the status of Northern Ireland in Article 1 as to other articles covered by the provisions for review under Article 11.

1. Interim changes

Even if there is no immediate prospect of securing active unionist participation in the working of the new relationships established under the Agreement, there are a number of changes in practice and procedure which might help improve the working of the Conference and a number of ways in which the meaning of the current Agreement might be clarified. Some formal amendments or additions to the terms of the Agreement, by way of a protocol or otherwise, would in itself be no bad thing, since it would alert unionists and others to the fact that both Governments recognise that the provisions adopted in 1985 are neither perfect nor fixed for all time.

(i) *The working of the Conference (Articles 2 and 3)*

One of the main drawbacks of the current practices and procedures of the Conference has been the atmosphere of secrecy and intrigue which has surrounded its operations. This has increased the opportunities for misrepresentation by the opponents of the Agreement and done little for the public reputation of the Conference as a vehicle for progress. It would be desirable for the agenda of the Conference on major issues to be made public well in advance of its regular ministerial meetings and for views and proposals from other interested parties to be invited. It would also be desirable for working papers and joint studies to be published, both to demonstrate the positive work carried out by the Conference and its Secretariat and to assist in gaining public support for the underlying objectives of the Agreement. The Anglo-Irish Joint Studies of 1981 were published in full as parliamentary papers in both jurisdictions. There is no good reason why many of the working papers of the Conference should not be similarly dealt with, even if agreement cannot be reached on every item in them. The fact that some issues, notably those involving operational decisions on security, must remain confidential should not be taken as a reason for confidentiality on all other matters. Publication of such documents as the programme of work for co-operation between the two police forces, provided for under Article 7, and studies by experts on the development of procedures for mixed courts, extra-territorial jurisdiction and extradition, as provided for under Article 8, should be seriously considered. Similar studies might be made and published on many of the issues covered in Article 5, such as ways of recognising and accommodating the rights and interests of the two communities in Northern Ireland and the protection of human rights.

Amendment of the terms of Articles 2 and 3 would not be essential for this purpose. But given the detailed description of procedure in Article 3 it would not be inappropriate to add the following provisions:

> The agenda of the meetings of the Conference at ministerial level shall be published in advance and views and proposals from other interested parties shall be invited as appropriate. Working papers and studies produced for the Conference shall be published as appropriate.

(ii) *Clarification on co-operative and reciprocal action (Articles 2, 5 and 8)*

There is a good deal of confusion, as explained in the detailed annotation above, on the precise role of the Conference in respect of co-operative and reciprocal action in Ireland and in Great Britain. It would be desirable to clarify the terms of the relevant provisions in Article 2 so that the jurisdiction and role of the Conference on such matters as the protection of the rights and interests of minorities in Ireland and of people of Irish origin in Britain, for example in respect of concern over the outcome of some terrorist trials in Britain, would be specified. This would assist in emphasising that while the primary concern of the Conference is in respect of Northern Ireland it is also concerned with the totality of relationships between Britain and Ireland, and particularly those which arise out of the conflict in Northern Ireland.

The following additions to Article 2 might be appropriate for this purpose, pending a more fundamental recasting of the Agreement as suggested below:

> *Co-operative and reciprocal action in Ireland and Great Britain shall be directed primarily at issues arising directly or indirectly from the conflict in Northern Ireland.*

It may also be appropriate to insert in Article 5(b) and Article 8 the following provisions to clarify the main concerns of the Conference in these respects:

> *Matters to be considered in this area shall include measures to enhance protection of human rights and to recognise and protect the rights and interests of minorities in Ireland.*

> *The two Governments agree on the importance of public confidence in the administration of justice in Northern Ireland, and in Ireland and Great Britain in relation to cases arising out of the conflict in Northern Ireland.*

(iii) *Clarification of main concerns for immediate future (Article 5)*

Some of the provisions of the current Agreement make reference to matters of particular concern in 1985 which have now been dealt with, such as changes in electoral arrangements and the use of flags and emblems in Article 5(a). It may be appropriate to remove these references and to insert some other issues of more current concern, such as the use of the Irish language and provisions for the funding of educational provision in Northern Ireland which will meet the wishes not only of both communities separately but also of those who wish to join in integrated schools, as follows:

> *Matters to be considered in this area include measures to foster the cultural heritage of both traditions, support for the Irish language, the provision of education for members of both communities and traditions both separately and together, the avoidance of economic and social discrimination and the advantages and disadvantages of a Bill of Rights in some form in Northern Ireland.*

(iv) *Composition of bodies (Article 6)*

The Police Complaints Board has been superseded by the Independent Commission for Police Complaints for Northern Ireland. This might be recognised in any revision of the Agreement.

(v) *Arrangements for review (Article 11)*

It would be desirable to make express provision for a further review of the working of the Conference at the end of a further period of its operation. The following provision may be appropriate:

> *At the end of three years from the completion of the initial review under this Article, or earlier if requested by either Government, a further review of the working of the Conference shall be undertaken to see whether any changes in the scope and nature of its activities are desirable.*

(vi) *Interparliamentary relations (Article 12)*

It would be desirable to make express provision for the form and functions of an Anglo-Irish Parliamentary body. Pending final agreement on current proposals it would not be appropriate to suggest a precise formulation of its composition here. It would also be desirable to make express provisions for such a body to scrutinise the implementation of the Agreement and the working of the Conference on a continuing basis and for the two Governments to commit themselves to co-operate with any such inter-parliamentary scrutiny along the following lines:

> *The primary role of (such a body) shall be to monitor progress in the implementation of this Agreement and in the working of the Conference. The two Governments shall co-operate with the work of the (body) by providing such information as it may require, giving evidence before it and giving such other support as may be appropriate.*

2. Accommodating full unionist participation

If there is a prospect of more active unionist participation in the working of the new Anglo-Irish structures then some more far-reaching changes in the Agreement are likely to be necessary. It would not be appropriate in advance of the negotiations which would be involved in any such recasting of the Agreement to make specific suggestions for the wording of new provisions. But it would probably be desirable to develop the Agreement in the following broad areas.

(i) *Status of Northern Ireland*

One of the primary concerns of unionists both before and after the signing of the Anglo-Irish Agreement has been the alleged claim in Articles 2 and 3 of the Irish Constitution over Northern Ireland. Unionists have argued with some justification that the provisions of Article 1 of the Anglo-Irish Agreement leave the alleged claim intact since reference is made only to changes in the status of Northern Ireland rather than to what its current status is. If unionists are to participate fully in any new structures, there is likely to be a need for more explicit recognition of the current status of Northern Ireland as part of the United Kingdom and therefore for a change in Articles 2 and 3 of the Irish Constitution to reflect the aspiration for Irish unity by consent rather than a claim to jurisdiction over Northern Ireland. The most appropriate development of Article 1 would perhaps be to add a provision binding both States to adopt in their internal constitutional legislation a parallel statement as to the current status of Northern Ireland as part of the United Kingdom of Great Britain and Northern Ireland and the principle of formal consent to any change. The provisions of Article 1 of the Agreement could thus be left intact. It should be noted that recent opinion polls in Ireland have indicated clearly that a majority of respondents in practice regard Irish unity as a long term aspiration rather than a realistic claim: for example an MRBI poll for the *Irish Times* in May and June 1987 indicated that while 67 per cent. of respondents regarded reunification as something to hope for, 49 per cent. thought it would never happen, and only 16 per cent. that it would happen within 25 years (*Irish Times*, September 1, 1987). These findings indicate that in the right political climate, such as an agreed reformulation of the Anglo-Irish Agreement with unionist participation, there would be clear majority support for the reformulation of Articles 2 and 3 of the Irish Constitution.

(ii) *Arrangements for the government of Northern Ireland*

Unionist consent to a revised Agreement is also likely to be dependent on the provision of more satisfactory and stable arrangements for the government of Northern Ireland, both under direct rule and in the event of devolution, than are currently included in the Agreement. The current method of legislating for Northern Ireland by way of Orders in Council is clearly unsatisfactory. Though draft proposals for Orders are usually circulated for comment, once they have been formally laid before Parliament they cannot be amended in any way. Northern Ireland MPs therefore have virtually no effective influence on the form of legislation affecting only Northern Ireland. It would not be impossible, pending agreement on devolution or for Orders on matters which have not yet been devolved, for special provisions to be made for the consideration and amendment of Northern Ireland Orders by a select committee prior to their final approval or rejection by motions in both Houses. The provisions for devolution under the Northern Ireland Constitution Act 1973 and the Northern Ireland Act 1982 may also require some amendment since they provide no guarantee that members representing the majority or the minority community may not at any time and on wholly unjustified grounds decide to withdraw from a power-sharing administration and thus threaten the whole structure for devolution. It would make for greater stability if formal protections and guarantees on matters of special concern to the minority, such as education and the location of industrial development, were provided by way of weighted majority requirements or entrenched constitutional rights. This would provide scope for the development of informal conventions on power-sharing within government without requiring continuing agreement on all matters as a condition of the continuance of devolved government.

(iii) *The totality of relationships*

It would also be desirable to spell out more clearly the role of the Conference in respect of the three main dimensions of Anglo-Irish relations: the internal Northern Ireland dimension, the North-South dimension (relationships between the two parts of Ireland), and the East-West dimension (relationships between Ireland and the United Kingdom as a whole). Under the existing Agreement the general relationships between the United Kingdom and Ireland are notionally covered under the auspices of the Anglo-Irish Intergovernmental Council established in 1981 while those relating specifically to Northern Ireland and to North-South relations are covered by the Anglo-Irish Intergovernmental Conference established under the Agreement in 1985. But there are no formal or detailed provisions setting out the precise jurisdiction and role of the Council. Rather than attempting to create a new and detailed agreement to govern East-West relations, it would be simpler to retain the general structure of the Conference, as provided in Articles 2 and 3 of the current Agreement, and to extend its jurisdiction to cover prescribed matters in respect of East-West relations. This could readily be achieved by extending potential membership of the Conference to all British and Irish ministers as appropriate and adding a new article or set of articles to govern the jurisdiction of the expanded Conference in respect of matters of concern to the United Kingdom as a whole and Ireland but without a specific Northern Ireland connection. For example, provision might be made for the discussion of arrangements for the free travel area and the control of aliens, for the development of a common approach to the protection of human rights by establishing appropriate agencies in each jurisdiction, and perhaps for the incorporation of Anglo-Irish Encounter within the framework of the Conference. The creation of an interparliamentary body of the kind envisaged in Article 12 of the current Agreement would also fit readily into an expanded Agreement of this kind.

In this way the role of the Conference would be expanded to cover the totality of relationships between Britain and Ireland, as was envisaged in the summit meeting between Mrs Thatcher and Mr. Haughey in 1981, without abandoning the more specific objectives in respect of Northern Ireland which were finally agreed in 1985. In one sense this would amount to little more than the formalisation of the existing close relationships between the British and Irish Governments on many matters of shared concern. But a development of the Agreement along these lines would make it easier for unionists to agree to participate fully in the new institutions, since a number of their leaders, notably Mr. Molyneaux, have suggested that an approach based on the Anglo-Irish Intergovernmental Council could be acceptable.

(iv) *An expanded Secretariat*
In this context it would be desirable to provide for the expansion and possible relocation of the Conference Secretariat to cover all three dimensions of Anglo-Irish relations. A permanent joint Secretariat could thus be maintained in London and Dublin as well as in Belfast. This too would help to meet unionist concerns about the location of the existing Secretariat at Maryfield without abandoning the real benefits to both Governments of maintaining a joint office to deal informally with matters of actual or potential political conflict and to exchange information on particular incidents or issues of immediate concern.

.　　.　　.　　.　　.　　.

A recasting of the Agreement along these broader lines would help to remind all the people of Britain and Ireland that the enterprise initiated in 1981 by Mr. Haughey and Mrs Thatcher was intended to provide for the totality of relationships between Great Britain and Ireland. It would assist greatly in securing the full participation of unionists in the new institutions. In so doing it would provide a renewed opportunity to achieve peace, stability and reconciliation in and over Northern Ireland as a unique frontier zone between two member states of the European Community. And as in the case of the European Community it would not be necessary to prescribe in advance how the new relationships and institutions would develop in the future.

CHAPTER 7

THE OFFICIAL REVIEW OF THE AGREEMENT

The following is the full text of the Review carried out under Article 11 of the Agreement, as published on May 24, 1989.

1. In accordance with Article 11 of the Anglo-Irish Agreement, the two Governments have completed a review of the working of the Intergovernmental Conference and have considered whether any changes in the scope and nature of its activities are desirable. In conducting this review the two sides engaged in an assessment of the work of the Conference to date under each of the Articles of the Agreement and examined the overall achievements of the Conference in terms of the stated objectives of the Agreement and the relationship between the two countries. Their discussions took account of a range of views put to them by interested groups and individuals and they wish to place on record their appreciation of all submissions made to them on the review. The conclusions which the two Governments have reached are set out below in the order in which the various subjects are covered by the Agreement.

2. Having conducted the review, the two Governments reaffirm their full commitment to all of the provisions of the Agreement and to the shared understandings and purposes set out both in the preamble and in the Agreement itself as well as in the Hillsborough Communiqué of 15 November 1985. They reaffirm their belief in the need for political dialogue at all levels, as an essential element in achieving progress and an end to violence. They reiterate their unyielding opposition to any attempt to promote political objectives by violence or the threat of violence; and they commit themselves to continuing close co-operation in the security field to ensure that those who resort to such methods do not succeed.

The Conference

3. The Intergovernmental Conference has met on twenty-seven occasions since the signature of the Agreement. It has provided a valuable forum to address in a regular and organised way the full range of matters covered in the Agreement, mainly affecting Northern Ireland, and to promote cooperative action in both parts of Ireland. Through the Conference, the Irish Government have put forward views and proposals on these issues for consideration by the British side. Thus, in the development of measures relating to Northern Ireland the Conference has played an important role, and both Governments look forward to working closely together in this way in the future along the lines laid down in the Agreement. They acknowledge the valuable contribution of the Secretariat in servicing the Conference and in providing a readily available and continuing channel of communication between the two Governments on matters covered by the Agreement, a role which they will seek to develop as appropriate.

4. With a view to improving the working of the Conference as a means of resolving differences between them, both Governments agree that Conference meetings in the future should be organised so far as possible on a regular schedule, following the pattern in 1988 when ten meetings were held. In addition to meeting the needs of the regular work of the Conference, this pattern should give both sides an opportunity to consider forthcoming developments on a systematic basis, thereby making it more likely that problems can be anticipated and resolved in the spirit of harmony called for by the Agreement and reducing the risk of misunderstanding or confrontation arising from particular events. In the interest of ensuring the

fullest possible consideration of longer-term issues relevant to the agenda of the Conference, it was also agreed that at least once each year there will be an informal Ministerial meeting.

5. Consistent with their objective of developing the potential of the Conference as envisaged in Article 3 of the Agreement, both Governments agree in principle that future Conference meetings should provide for widened Ministerial participation, at the invitation of the Joint Chairmen, to encourage more structured discussion of a greater range of issues of common interest to both parts of Ireland.

6. The two Governments note that a number of the submissions which they have received emphasise the importance of fuller information about discussions at Conference meetings being made public. Both Governments agree that the public should be made fully aware of the contribution which the work of the Conference is making and will seek to respond to this point in future communiqués and press conferences.

Devolution

7. It continues to be the British Government's policy, supported by the Irish Government, to encourage progress towards the devolution of responsibility for certain powers to elected representatives in Northern Ireland as set out in Article 4 of the Agreement. Both sides recognise that the achievement of devolution depends on the cooperation of constitutional representatives of both traditions within Northern Ireland.

Accommodation of the rights and identities of the two traditions

8. The two Governments share a common view of the central importance in the implementation of the Agreement of measures to accommodate the rights and identities of the two traditions in Northern Ireland, to protect human rights and prevent discrimination. The Irish Government welcome a number of positive measures which have been implemented by the British Government in this respect since the signature of the Agreement. These include the repeal of the Flags and Emblems Act, the enfranchisement of the "I Voters" and the enactment of the Public Order (NI) Order 1987 enhancing the powers of the police to control potentially provocative marches.

9. The introduction of new legislation on fair employment has been the subject of detailed discussion in the Conference in the light of the commitment to eliminate discrimination in the workplace and establish fair employment practices in Northern Ireland. The two Governments agree on the importance of ensuring that such legislation shall be an effective means of meeting that commitment and the Conference will closely follow developments in this regard. The Irish Government welcome also the launching by the British Government of a programme of action to address the social and economic problems in the most disadvantaged areas of Belfast and other deprived areas.

10. Both Governments reaffirm the fundamental importance of the proper protection of human rights and will continue to discuss through the mechanism of the Conference all legislative and other means by which such rights may be better protected in Northern Ireland.

11. The two Governments attach importance to the continuing work for improved community relations through developing increased cross-community contact and cooperation, and to encouraging greater mutual understanding including respecting the cultural heritage of both traditions. They recognise the valuable role which the education system can play in promoting mutual esteem and understanding between the two traditions, and the Irish Government support the efforts made to reflect this objective in the new curriculum for Northern Ireland currently under preparation.

The two Governments recognise also the importance of the Irish language in this context and undertake to support efforts to enhance awareness and appreciation of this particular strand of the cultural heritage.

Public bodies

12. The two Governments agree on the importance of the principle that public bodies in Northern Ireland should be so constituted as to enjoy the widest possible respect and acceptance throughout the community. Exchanges will continue on ways in which this objective can be furthered. The Irish Government will continue to put forward views and proposals on the role and composition of such bodies for consideration by the British side, which will be ready to consider what means may be available to remedy imbalances arising from the use by others of their existing nominating powers without due regard to fairness or balance.

Confidence in the security forces and the system of justice

13. The two Governments attach great importance to policies aimed at improving relations between the security forces and the community in Northern Ireland and at enhancing respect for the rule of law. They have considered the record of the working of the Conference in relation to fostering confidence in the system of justice in all its aspects and ensuring that the security forces are clearly perceived to discharge their duties even-handedly, acting at all times within the law, with equal respect for the unionist and nationalist traditions and with demonstrable accountability for their actions. Special importance is attached to ensuring that representations by the public about the behaviour of members of the security forces are promptly and fully addressed and, in particular, that any allegations of harassment are quickly investigated and that, if complaints are substantiated, the necessary action is taken without delay.

14. A number of new measures affecting these confidence issues has [*sic*] been introduced, including those on marches and other public events, incitement to hatred, police complaints procedures, police/community liaison committees and the need for the police to respect equally the two traditions in Northern Ireland which is set out in the Code of Conduct promulgated by the Royal Ulster Constabulary. Further work remains to be done and progress achieved will be reviewed on a regular basis at the Conference.

15. Following discussion in the Conference, further confidence-building measures are envisaged or in hand by the relevant authorities, including the following: systematic monitoring of the nature, pattern and handling of complaints by the public about the behaviour of members of the security forces; further effective development of the policy of ensuring as rapidly as possible that, save in the most exceptional circumstances, there should be a police presence in all operations which involve direct contact between the armed forces and the community; additional safeguards for members of the public being questioned by the police in connection with non-terrorist offences; and the publication of a guide to the operation of the provisions of the Emergency Provisions and Prevention of Terrorism Acts.

16. The Irish Government reaffirm the importance they attach to reform of the system of trial under the Emergency Provisions Act 1978 and in particular the introduction of three-judge courts. The British Government are not at present persuaded of the merits of this proposal. While it is recognised that emergency legislation was a response to the campaign of violence and intimidation, it is agreed that both sides will continue through the Conference to consider what changes may be desirable in the emergency

provisions, the general criminal law or procedure with the aim of securing maximum public confidence in the system of justice.

17. The Conference has considered prisons policy. There have been important developments affecting the Northern Ireland prison system, including the special reviews of the cases of the remaining prisoners in special category and those serving sentences at the Secretary of State's pleasure, as well as life sentence review procedures generally, the opening of the new prison at Maghaberry, and matters affecting the prison regime. The two Governments undertake to maintain exchanges on prison matters, given the importance of careful and considered treatment of this sensitive issue.

18. The two Governments are fully agreed on the need for fair and effective procedures for extradition and for the exercise of extra-territorial jurisdiction to ensure that fugitive offenders are brought to justice. There has been extensive discussion of these matters within the framework of the Conference. The two Governments will continue their examination of these matters, through their respective Law Officers and the mechanism of the Conference, with a view to ensuring that appropriate arrangements are in place in relation both to extradition and extra-territorial jurisdiction.

19. The two Governments agree that there should be further study of areas of the criminal law applying in the two jurisdictions which might with benefit be harmonised.

Security cooperation

20. The two Governments condemn in the strongest terms the actions of those who in seeking to promote political ends by violent means cause the most callous loss of life, human misery and wanton destruction. They reaffirm their determination to counter this evil through continuing close cooperation between the security forces on both sides of the border and pay tribute to the commitment of these forces. Cross-border security cooperation has received regular and intensive consideration at meetings within the framework of the Intergovernmental Conference as well as at frequent meetings between the respective police forces. A programme of work between the Commissioner of the Garda Siochana and the Chief Constable of the Royal Ulster Constabulary as envisaged in Article 9 of the Agreement was put in hand and substantial progress has been achieved under all of the headings listed.

21. In the light of their common understanding of the scale of the terrorist threat, the two Governments reaffirm their commitment to further and sustained efforts to combat it effectively. They have endorsed a programme of future work between the two police forces to develop their cooperation and to enhance their capacity to protect human life and property from terrorist outrage. They agree that progress in cross-border security cooperation will be reviewed regularly by the Conference which the two Governments will continue to use as a framework to work together to ensure that those who adopt or support violence do not succeed.

Cross-border economic cooperation

22. The two Governments have taken stock of the pattern of cross-border economic cooperation since the signature of the Agreement. Apart from the work of the Conference itself a number of cross-border Ministerial meetings has [sic] taken place in the framework of the Agreement and a cross-border study of social and economic problems in the North West region has been commissioned with assistance from the European Community. The two Governments affirm their conviction that cross-border economic and social cooperation is of obvious benefit to all.

23. They agree that future Conference meetings will include a systematic programme of assessment of all the main sectors to determine where the process of cooperation can most fruitfully be expanded. Where appropriate, the responsible Ministers North and South will participate in the work of the Conference. In a preliminary survey during the review, both Governments have considered an illustrative list of areas which offer scope for further work, including transport, communications, tourism, industry, agriculture, energy and health.

24. The two Governments have considered also the implications of the completion of the internal market in the European Community in 1992. They recognise that these will be far-reaching and will generate common opportunities for both parts of Ireland as well as common difficulties arising from peripheral island status and other factors including the increase of competition. They agree that the Conference could provide a valuable forum for both sides to consider and assess the cross-border implications of the Single European Market and, consistent with national policies, to maximise the potential benefits. Various practical ways of advancing work in this area will be considered and the continuation of the dialogue on this issue begun at Louvain in December 1988 will also be encouraged.

International Fund for Ireland

25. In September 1986 the two Governments, in accordance with Article 10(a) of the Agreement, established the International Fund for Ireland with the financial support of the United States, Canada and New Zealand and, from 1989, the European Community. In the interval since its foundation the Fund has committed over £50m Sterling to projects in Northern Ireland and the border counties in the South and has been instrumental in creating a significant number of new jobs. The two Governments express their appreciation of the generosity of the donors to the Fund and will continue to give every support to the work of the Fund and the emphasis it is now placing on improving the position in the most disadvantaged areas.

British-Irish Interparliamentary Body

26. The two Governments welcome the progress which has been made towards the establishment of a British-Irish Interparliamentary Body of the kind envisaged in the Anglo-Irish Studies Report of November 1981, which would provide a valuable independent forum for interparliamentary contacts.

Conclusion

27. The two Governments commit themselves to continue to work together through the institutions and procedures of the Agreement for the realisation of the fundamental objectives of promoting peace and stability in Northern Ireland; helping to diminish the divisions between the two major traditions in Ireland; creating a new climate of friendship and cooperation between them and improving cooperation in combatting terrorism. Reaffirming the right of each tradition to pursue its aspirations by peaceful and constitutional means, they reiterate the objective of the creation of a society in Northern Ireland in which all may live in peace, free from discrimination and intolerance.

28. They agree that the Conference, together with its related mechanisms, has proved its value to both Governments in the three years since the signature of the Agreement and that, while requiring no fundamental change at present, its role could nevertheless be developed and enhanced in the ways set out above.

29. If in future it were to appear that the objectives of the Agreement could be more effectively served by changes in the scope and nature of the working of the Conference, consistent with the basic provisions and spirit of the Agreement, the two Governments would be ready in principle to consider such changes.

30. The two Governments stress that the Agreement does not represent a threat to either tradition in Northern Ireland. On the contrary, it provides a framework which respects the essential interests of both sides of the community and their right to pursue their aspirations by peaceful means. It facilitates cooperation in the fight against terrorism and sets out to create the conditions in which the whole communiy can live together in peace.

May 24, 1989

INDEX

ACHIEVEMENTS,
  economic co-operation, 75
  generally, 72–73
  Intergovernmental Conference, 74
  legal matters, 74–75
  peace, 73
  political matters, 74
  reconciliation, 73
  security matters, 75
  stability, 73
ADMINISTRATION OF JUSTICE,
  annotation of Agreement, 38–40
  confidence in, 85–86
  general structure of Agreement, 10
ADVISORY COMMITTEE,
  International Fund for Ireland, 56
AGREEMENT. See ANGLO-IRISH AGREEMENT,
AGRICULTURE,
  cross-border co-operation, 44
ALLIANCE. See LIBERAL/SOCIAL DEMOCRATIC
    PARTY ALLIANCE,
ANGLO-IRISH AGREEMENT,
  achievements. See ACHIEVEMENTS,
  annotation. See ANNOTATION OF
    AGREEMENT,
  background. See BACKGROUND TO
    AGREEMENT,
  entry into force, 1
  future developments. See FUTURE
    DEVELOPMENTS,
  general structure. See GENERAL
    STRUCTURE OF AGREEMENT,
  generally, 9
  House of Commons, motion of support
    passed by, 1
  House of Lords, motion of support passed
    by, 1
  Ireland, support from, 1
  momentum, restoration of, 77–78
  objectives, 76–77
  official review. See OFFICIAL REVIEW OF
    AGREEMENT,
  parties, 1
  reactions to. See REACTIONS TO
    AGREEMENT
  signing, 1
  status. See STATUS OF AGREEMENT,
  United Nations, lodged at, 1
ANGLO-IRISH ENCOUNTER,
  establishment of, 5
  half yearly conferences, 5–6
  proceedings, 6
ANGLO-IRISH INTERGOVERNMENTAL COUNCIL,
  creation of, 5

ANGLO-IRISH INTERGOVERNMENTAL COUNCIL
    —cont.
  meetings, 5
  See also INTERGOVERNMENTAL
    CONFERENCE,
ANGLO-IRISH JOINT STUDIES OF 1981,
  developments, 4–5
ANNOTATION OF AGREEMENT,
  administration of justice, 38–40
  cross-border co-operation, 40–46
  cultural matters, cross-border co-
    operation on, 40–46
  economic matters, cross-border co-
    operation on, 40–46
  final clauses, 48
  Intergovernmental Conference,
    establishment of, 22–26
    functions, 28–30
    meetings, 26–28
    objectives, 28–30
  International Fund for Ireland, 51–58
  legal matters, 38–40
  Northern Ireland, status of, 18–22
  parliamentary relations, 47–48
  parties, 15
  political matters, 30–35
  Preamble, 15–18
  review, arrangements for, 46–47
  security matters, 35–38, 40–46
  social matters, cross-border co-operation
    on, 40–46
ANNUAL REPORT,
  International Fund for Ireland, 56
ARTS,
  cross-border co-operation, 45
AUDITORS,
  International Fund for Ireland, 56

BACKGROUND TO AGREEMENT,
  Anglo-Irish Encounter, 5–6
  Anglo-Irish Intergovernmental Council, 5
  Anglo-Irish Joint Studies of 1981, 4–5
  conflicting claims, 1–2
  New Ireland Forum,
    Alliance report, 7–8
    British Government reaction, 7
    generally, 6–7
    Kilbrandon Report, 7–8
    Unionist responses, 8
  preparation, 8–9
  Sunningdale Conference,
    Council of Ireland, 2–3
    failure of package, 3–4
    generally, 2

BACKGROUND TO AGREEMENT—*cont.*
  Sunningdale Conference—*cont.*
    Northern Ireland, status of, 2
    power-sharing Executive, 3
    terrorism, co-operation on, 3
BOARD,
  International Fund for Ireland. *See*
    INTERNATIONAL FUND FOR IRELAND,
BRITISH-IRISH INTERPARLIAMENTARY BODY,
  establishment of, 87

CO-OPERATION,
  annotation of Agreement, 40–46
  general structure of Agreement, 10
  interim changes, 79
  Official Review of Agreement, 86–87
  terrorism, on, Sunningdale agreement on,
    3
COMMUNITY RELATIONS,
  International Fund for Ireland, activities
    of, 50
CONFERENCE. *See* INTERGOVERNMENTAL
    CONFERENCE,
CONSTITUTION,
  conflicting claims, 1–2
COUNCIL OF IRELAND,
  Sunningdale agreement on, 2–3
CROSS-BORDER CO-OPERATION. *See* CO-
    OPERATION,
CULTURAL MATTERS,
  cross-border co-operation,
    annotation of Agreement, 40–46
    general structure of Agreement, 10

DEVOLUTION,
  Official Review of Agreement, 84
DISTURBANCES,
  outbreak of, in 1968, 1

ECONOMIC MATTERS,
  achievements of Agreement, 75
  cross-border co-operation,
    annotation of Agreement, 40–46
    general structure of Agreement, 10
EDUCATION,
  cross-border co-operation, 44
ENVIRONMENT,
  cross-border co-operation, 44
EUROPEAN CONVENTION ON SUPPRESSION OF
    TERRORISM,
  implementation, 64
  offences, 63–64
EXTRA-TERRITORIAL JURISDICTION,
  Sunningdale compromise on, 60–61
EXTRADITION,
  European Convention on Suppression of
    Terrorism, 63–64
  extra-territorial jurisdiction, Sunningdale
    compromise on, 60–61
  Irish legislation on, 64–66
  overlapping stages, 59
  political offence exemption,
    judicial re-interpretation, 61–63
    strict application of, 59–60

FAIR EMPLOYMENT AGENCY,
  role and composition of, 34–35
FINAL CLAUSES,
  annotation of Agreement, 48
  general structure of Agreement, 10
FISHERIES,
  cross-border co-operation, 44
FUTURE DEVELOPMENTS,
  generally, 76
  interim changes,
    co-operation and reciprocal action,
      clarification on, 79
    composition of bodies, 79
    Conference, working of, 78
    generally, 78
    immediate future, clarification of main
      concerns for, 79
    interparliamentary relations, 80
    review, arrangements for, 79–80
  momentum of Agreement, restoration of,
    77–78
  objectives of Agreement, 76–77
  unionist participation, increase in,
    expanded Secretariat, 82
    generally, 80
    Northern Ireland,
      government of, arrangements for, 81
      status of, 80
    totality of relationships, 81–82

GENERAL STRUCTURE OF AGREEMENT,
  administration of justice, 10
  complexity of, 10
  cross-border co-operation, 10
  cultural matters, cross-border co-
    operation on, 10
  economic matters, cross-border co-
    operation on, 10
  final clauses, 10
  generally, 9
  Intergovernmental Conference, 9–10
  interparliamentary relations, 10
  legal matters, 10
  Northern Ireland, status of, 9
  political matters, 10
  Preamble, 9
  review, arrangements for, 10
  security matters, 10
  social matters, cross-border co-operation
    on, 10
GRANTS,
  International Fund for Ireland, by, 54

HEALTH,
  cross-border co-operation, 44
HOUSE OF COMMONS,
  Anglo-Irish Agreement, motion of
    support for, 1
HOUSE OF LORDS,
  Anglo-Irish Agreement, motion of
    support for, 1

INDEPENDENT COMMISSION FOR POLICE
    COMPLAINTS FOR NORTHERN IRELAND,
  composition of, 79

Index

INFRASTRUCTURE,
cross-border co-operation, 44
INTERGOVERNMENTAL CONFERENCE,
achievements, 74
annotation of Agreement, 22–30
establishment of, 22–26
expanded Secretariat, 82
functions, 28–30
general structure of Agreement, 9–10
interim changes, 78
meetings, 26–28
objectives, 28–30
Official Review of Agreement, 83–84
totality of relationships, 81–82
INTERNATIONAL FUND FOR IRELAND,
administration, 49
agreement,
amendment of, 56
entry into force, 56–57
annotation of Agreement, 51–58
basis of, 49
Board,
Advisory Committee, establishment of,
56
Annual Report, 56
assistance, applications for, 54
auditors, appointment of, 56
composition, 54
membership, 49
procedure, 54
community relations, 50
establishment of, 49, 51
further Agreement, amendment by, 56
international organisation, as, 53
investment companies, establishment of,
55
legal personality, 53
major programmes of work, 49–50
objectives, 51–52
Official Review of Agreement, 87
priorities and policies, 50
progress of, 57–58
resources, disbursement of, 50
value for money basis, 52–53
venture capital, 54–55
INTERNATIONAL LAW,
status of Agreement in,
generally, 11
Vienna Convention, 11–12
INTERNATIONAL ORGANISATION,
International Fund for Ireland as, 53
INTERPARLIAMENTARY RELATIONS,
annotation of Agreement, 47–48
general structure of Agreement, 10
interim changes, 80
INVESTMENT COMPANIES,
International Fund for Ireland,
establishment by, 55
IRELAND,
Anglo-Irish Agreement, support for, 1
extradition, legislation on, 64–66
International Fund for. *See*
INTERNATIONAL FUND FOR IRELAND
opinion polls, 72

IRELAND—*cont.*
peace-keeping force in Northern Ireland,
request for, 1–2
reaction to Agreement, 67–69

JOINT STUDIES,
cross-border co-operation, 45
JURISDICTION,
extra-territorial, Sunningdale compromise
on, 60–61
JUSTICE. *See* ADMINISTRATION OF JUSTICE,

KILBRANDON COMMITTEE,
New Ireland Forum, response to, 7–8

LEGAL MATTERS,
achievements of Agreement, 74–75
annotation of Agreement, 38–40
general structure of Agreement, 10
LIBERAL/SOCIAL DEMOCRATIC PARTY
ALLIANCE,
New Ireland Forum, response to, 7–8
LOANS,
International Fund for Ireland, by, 54

NATIONAL LAW,
status of Agreement in, 12–14
NEW IRELAND FORUM,
establishment of, 6
Report,
Alliance report, 7–8
British Government reaction, 7
conclusions, 6–7
Kilbrandon Report, 7–8
Unionist responses, 8
NORTHERN IRELAND,
government arrangements for, 81
opinion polls, 72
reaction to Agreement, 69–71
status of,
accommodating full unionist
participation, 80
annotation of Agreement, 18–22
general structure of Agreement, 9
Sunningdale agreement on, 2

OFFENCE,
extradition. *See* EXTRADITION,
OFFICIAL REVIEW OF AGREEMENT,
British-Irish Interparliamentary Body, 87
co-operation,
cross-border economic, 86–87
security, 86
Conference, 83–84
devolution, 84
full text, 83–88
generally, 83
International Fund for Ireland, 87
justice, confidence in system of, 85–86
public bodies, 85
security,
co-operation, 86
forces, confidence in, 85–86
traditions, accommodation of rights and
identities of, 84–85

91

OPINION POLLS,
generally, 71–72
Ireland, 72
Northern Ireland, 72

PARTIES,
descriptions of, differences in, 1, 15
PEACE,
achievements of Agreement, 73
PEACE-KEEPING FORCE,
Irish Government, request by, 1–2
POLICE AUTHORITY FOR NORTHERN IRELAND,
role and composition of, 34–35
POLICE COMPLAINTS BOARD,
composition of, 79
role and composition of, 34–35
POLITICAL OFFENCE EXCEPTION,
judicial re-interpretation of, 61–63
strict application of, 59–60
POLITICS,
achievements of Agreement, 74
annotation of Agreement, 30–35
general structure of Agreement, 10
nature of Agreement, 14
POWER-SHARING EXECUTIVE,
Sunningdale agreement on, 3
PREAMBLE,
general structure, 9
PUBLIC BODIES,
Official Review of Agreement, 85

REACTIONS TO AGREEMENT,
political,
Britain, in, 67
generally, 67
Ireland, in, 67–69
Northern Ireland, in, 69–71
talks about talks, 71
RECIPROCITY,
interim changes, 79
RECONCILIATION,
achievements of Agreement, 73
REVIEW,
arrangements for,
annotation of Agreement, 46–47
general structure of Agreement, 10
interim changes, 79–80
Official. *See* OFFICIAL REVIEW OF
AGREEMENT,

SECURITY,
achievements of Agreement, 75
annotation of Agreement, 35–38
cross-border co-operation,
annotation of Agreement, 40–46
general structure of Agreement, 10
Official Review of Agreement, 86
forces, confidence in, 85–86
general structure of Agreement, 10
SERVICES,
cross-border co-operation, 44
SOCIAL MATTERS,
cross-border co-operation,
annotation of Agreement, 40–46

SOCIAL MATTERS—*cont.*
cross-border co-operation—*cont.*
general structure of Agreement, 10
SOCIAL SECURITY,
cross-border co-operation, 44
SPORT,
cross-border co-operation, 45
STABILITY,
achievements of Agreement, 73
STANDING ADVISORY COMMISSION ON HUMAN
RIGHTS,
role and composition of, 34–35
STATUS OF AGREEMENT,
international law,
generally, 11
Vienna Convention, 11–12
national law, 12–14
STATUS OF NORTHERN IRELAND. *See under*
NORTHERN IRELAND,
SUNNINGDALE CONFERENCE,
Council of Ireland, 2–3
extra-territorial jurisdiction, on, 60–61
failure of package, 3–4
generally, 2
Northern Ireland, status of, 2
power-sharing Executive, 3
terrorism, co-operation on, 3

TALKS ABOUT TALKS,
progress on, 71
TAXATION,
cross-border co-operation, 45
TERRORISM,
co-operation on, Sunningdale agreement
on, 3
European Convention on Suppression of,
63–64
TRADE,
freedom of, re-establishment of, 1
TRADITIONS,
rights and identities, accommodation of,
84–85
TRANSPORT,
cross-border co-operation, 44

UNIONISTS,
full participation,
expanded Secretariat, 82
generally, 80
Northern Ireland,
government, arrangements for, 81
status of, 80
totality of relationships, 81–82
New Ireland Forum, response to, 8
UNITED NATIONS,
Anglo-Irish Agreement lodged at, 1

VALUE FOR MONEY BASIS,
International Fund for Ireland, 52–53
VENTURE CAPITAL,
International Fund for Ireland,
contribution by, 54–55
VIENNA CONVENTION,
status of Agreement, 11–12